A typical Chinese meal

HELEN BURKE
in collaboration with FU TONG

CHINESE
cooking for pleasure

Preface by Fu Tong

PAUL HAMLYN

PHOTOGRAPHER Michael Holford
ILLUSTRATORS   Jill Mackley, Gay John Galsworthy
DESIGNER   Veronica Mathew

China by kind permission of Arts and Crafts of China

© Copyright Helen Burke 1965
First published 1965; Second impression 1968
Published by THE HAMLYN PUBLISHING GROUP LTD.
HAMLYN HOUSE · THE CENTRE · FELTHAM · MIDDLESEX
Printed in Czechoslovakia by Svoboda, Prague
T 1790

CONTENTS

PREFACE BY FU TONG

Confucius, in his infinite wisdom said of food, 'It is the first happiness.' As a Chinese, I am an ardent admirer of that great sage and of this philosophy in particular. I endorse his sympathies warm-heartedly. Food is my whole life — the shopping for it; its preparation; its cooking; the consuming of it; and the sense of satisfaction on reflecting a memorable repast. We Chinese take our eating seriously; no mere necessity — a means to provide the body with the bare essentials for existence. No trivial sandwich or snack to offset that irritating pang of hunger. Never! Food to my countrymen, is one of the ecstasies of life, to be thought about in advance; to be smothered with loving care throughout its preparation; and to have time lavished on it in the final pleasure of eating.

A meal in China can last for as long as four hours. It is a solemn ritual — the various courses punctuated by numerous cups of Jasmine tea, to aid digestion and give appetite for further delicacies to come.

As a child in Hong Kong, I was taught to respect food. In common with other children, I learned to use chopsticks which enable one to sample and savour from each bowl the subtle tastes and aromas of the exotic herbs and spices which are so much a part of Oriental cuisine.

In 1958, with the opening of FU TONG in London's Kensington, my ambition to open a restaurant and spread the cult of Chinese eating came true. From the outset, it was my policy to serve *only* Chinese food. Don't misunderstand; I am a devotee of typical English fare. It would, though, in my opinion, be folly to attempt to produce English food in my restaurant — so many establishments could present it so much better. FU TONG became rapidly established and soon I was in a position to spread my 'gospel' with new restaurants — the

KWAN YIN at Mill Hill, the FU TONG at Esher, Surrey and the TONG YEN in Paris. However, always at the back of my mind was one nagging thought — how to reach an even wider public?

Then, someone asked me to write a cookery book — the obvious answer; but alas, my experience was entirely practical. I had neither the ability nor the command of the English language to embark on such an exciting project.

It occurred to me at the time that the one person with whom I could co-operate in producing a cookery volume would be HELEN BURKE, one of Britain's foremost writers on cookery. I had met Helen, a delightful woman and enthusiastic gourmet, some years before when she came to dine with me to discuss an article on my restaurant for one of her Evening Standard features. With our mutual interest in food and all its aspects, we had talked for hours and become firm friends. I was delighted, therefore, when Helen, commissioned to write this book and feeling not altogether sure of the technicalities of Chinese cuisine, insisted that I be her collaborator. As the happiest of teams, we began our work. The result of our labours is here for your sharing. The art of Chinese cooking does not, contrary to popular belief, present any real difficulties. Basic English raw materials are easily mingled with Oriental herbs and spices now readily available in this country. Besides looking highly decorative and tasting superb, food prepared in the Chinese manner is also most nourishing, retaining as it does — with quick, minimum cooking — all its vitamin content.

It has given both my wife and myself the greatest pleasure to collaborate with Helen Burke. We hope that these pages may bring you active participation in that pleasure.

INTRODUCTION

When I was first asked to write a book of recipes of Chinese dishes, I must say that I was flattered — but I refused.

In doing so, I explained that, although I knew a fair amount about Chinese cookery, I did not know enough. Since a very early age, I had known and very much liked Chinese food.

On the coast of my native British Columbia, we had many Chinese people. There, as they do in most parts of the world where they settle, they established their own 'village' which inevitably, in the New World, at least, became known as 'China Town'.

In the city of Vancouver, for instance, we had a 'China Town' with shops selling every possible ingredient for Chinese dishes, authentic Chinese china and the most beautiful Chinese furniture and furnishings. And there were Chinese restaurants, of course. Incidentally, even in villages on Vancouver Island itself, there were 'China Towns'.

In my part of the west of Canada, there was any number of very good Chinese cooks in private service and many other people cooked certain Chinese dishes. My mother, herself a gifted cook, had learned much from these Chinese cooks and I, in due course, acquired a certain amount of knowledge and many helpful tips from her.

The need for everything to be on hand and ready at the outset; the need for careful preparation and, above all, the need for just enough cooking and no more. Indeed, the preparation takes longer than the cooking time. It is said, loosely, 90% preparation and 10% cooking.

These are the 'secrets' of the art of Chinese cookery.

All the ingredients for the dishes were readily available and the fact that the Chinese in Vancouver seemed to have a monopoly in market gardening (what we called 'truck gardening') meant that we had the most excellent vegetables and a greater variety of them than might otherwise have been possible.

Many of the ingredients in Chinese cookery — bamboo shoots, bean sprouts, water chestnuts and so on are, literally, foreign to us but all of them are obtainable in this country. Not only are there so called eastern 'emporiums' in London and other cities, but, thanks to the evergrowing interest in Chinese cookery, most of the London and provincial stores also stock a great variety of Oriental goods.

Finally, when I was again approached to write this book, I agreed to do so— provided I could have the help of Fu Tong of Kensington High Street whom I knew. By a happy coincidence, he, too, had a book in mind and, whereas I wanted his co-operation, it turned out that he wanted mine!

Here, then, is the book, written by me in collaboration with Fu Tong, Winnie his charming Chinese wife and their deft young Chinese chefs.

While the dishes in this book were prepared before my eyes by a Chinese chef in the kitchen of a Chinese restaurant, it was not always the same chef and not always the same kitchen. Indeed, the preparations were carried out in four different kitchens — those of Fu Tong in Kensington High Street and Esher, Kwan Yin in Mill Hill and Tong Yen in Paris.

Each was a first-class Chinese chef but each had his own ideas. One chef, for instance, would allow for more sauce than the others in dishes in which beef or chicken stock and cornflour were used. Another chef, in similar dishes, would use so little sauce as to end up with almost none at all.

We, like the chefs, can allow ourselves a certain latitude and be guided by our own likes in matters such as the consistency of a dish and its flavouring and seasoning.

HELEN BURKE

7

CHINESE EATING

The great difference between eating the Chinese way and, let us say, the Western way is that the Chinese use chopsticks and we use knives and forks — for main dishes, at any rate. This inevitably means that large pieces of fish, meat and poultry are not possible at the Chinese table. Most dishes, therefore, are made up of mouth-sized pieces which are taken up by chopsticks and transferred to the mouth.

For one main course of a Chinese meal, there may be as many as 5-6 different dishes — fish and/or shellfish, meat, poultry, vegetables, invariably including plainly boiled or fried rice.

Savoury sauces are also a feature of a Chinese meal. The three principal ones are chilli (which one can buy), mustard (much like the sauce that we ourselves make) and plum, which one can also buy. (These are illustrated in colour on the jacket). Small spoonsful of the chosen sauce are placed on one's plate. A morsel of the fish, shellfish, meat or poultry is taken up with chopsticks, dipped in sauce and eaten — or the other way about. The use of chopsticks determines the kind and size of the portions to be consumed.

Chinese food is deliciously tasty and the variety of flavours is so cleverly contained in each dish that there is nothing incongruous in the serving of fish, meat and poultry in the same course.

Far from being incongruous, this 'mixing of foods' means that both cooking and eating become pleasingly adventurous. And it is because more than one dish is served at one course that the quantities in the various recipes in this book are small.

There is an ever-increasing interest in and appreciation of Chinese food in this country. The fact that Chinese restaurants in Great Britain have grown from the comparatively few in the not-so-distant past to the thousands that exist today is ample testimony to the variety and quality of Chinese dishes. It would seem that nearly every week one reads of a new Chinese restaurant opening.

This book is intended for the beginner who would cook simply and well the 'Chinese way'. The quick-time cooking cannot but have a great appeal to the busy woman. Obviously, too, the speed of cooking means a considerable economy in fuel.

HOW TO USE CHOPSTICKS

As shown in figure 'A', hold first chopstick firm and stationary in fixed position.

As shown in figure 'B', second chopstick is held like a pencil, with the tips of thumb, index and second fingers. Manipulate this chopstick to meet the first chopstick.

As shown in figure 'C', this manipulation will form a vice to pick up your food.

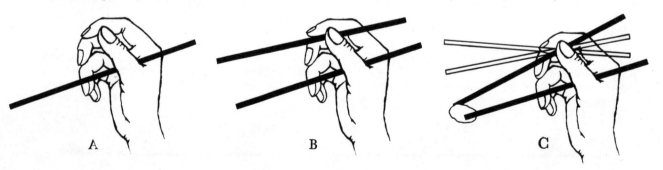

A   B   C

KITCHEN EQUIPMENT

Every dish in this book can be prepared and cooked with the equipment found in the normal home kitchen with, perhaps, a few smallish additions.

An ordinary frying-pan (a good wide one) can take the place of the Chinese 'wog'. This is a semi-sphere which requires a special application of heat.

The Chinese cook can first fry fish or meat or poultry or vegetables in his 'wog', then push it upwards and aside while preparing additional ingredients in the base of the vessel, keeping both apart. We, with our flat flying-pans, will fry the fish or other food and transfer it to a heated dish while carrying out the second preparation, or use another frying-pan.

A large frying-pan is much better than a small one because food can be tossed or turned, or both, in it without fear of spilling.

One of the best all-round cutting and chopping implements is a meat cleaver. I would suggest buying two of them. The ones I have in mind are something like a butcher's chopper, but much smaller. The blade will be about 3 inches wide and 7-8 inches long. At the sharp point, less than $\frac{1}{4}$ inch at its widest, it is razor-sharp.

These cleavers are very versatile. With one of them you can scrape the scales off fish or disjoint a raw chicken, cutting cleanly through the bones to make the mouth-sized pieces of chicken so much served in Chinese dishes. With two cleavers, one in each hand, you can cut meat or vegetables into wafer-thin pieces, doubly quick, of course, without losing any of their juices as you would do in a mincing-machine.

A wooden chopping block in the kitchen would be more than useful but a good thick meat-cutting board can stand in very well for it.

When it comes to deep-fat frying, a deep oval pot with a wire basket would be better than a round one, especially for those occasions when you want to deep-fat fry a good-sized fish or a whole duck, such as Cantonese duck (see page 68).

Other implements A long-handled flattish round skimmer, perforated or made of wire; a ladle which can also serve as a measure and a cup; one's ordinary fish slices, spatulas, colanders and sieves. When it comes to noodle nests (see page 116), do try to find a small frying-basket just wide enough in which to shape the noodles before deep-frying them. Such a basket will help you to make the 'nests' as professionally as do the Chinese cooks. For steaming foods, an ordinary steamer will do very well. I use a so-called 'waterless' cooker with a little water in it and a trivet on which to stand anything to be cooked this way. Cantonese duck, on page 68 is an example of this method of steaming.

WEIGHTS AND MEASURES

Weights throughout the book are given in lb. and oz. Capacity measure in Imperial pints and fractions thereof, with small amounts in spoon measures. For the benefit of American readers liquid ingredients have been given to the nearest U.S. standard cup measure. These follow the English measure i.e. 1 pint (U.S. 2½ cups).

In Britain all dry ingredients are weighed on a scale which registers ounces and pounds. To measure fractions of spoons use the small measures provided in measuring sets or divide the spoon. The American standard measuring spoons are slightly smaller in capacity than the British standard measuring spoons. The proportion, however, is similar in that 3 American standard teaspoons equal 1 tablespoon. Weights are not much used in Chinese cooking, especially in the professional kitchen. Occasionally, because it seemed the better way, weights have been given in some recipes but, for the most part, the measurements are given in 'spoons'. In each case, rounded tablespoons are implied.

Cornflour appears in most of the savoury dishes. It is given in rather meagre amounts because a thick sauce could spoil the dish. But if anyone prefers a thicker sauce, it is very easy to achieve. Simply increase the quantity of cornflour given in the recipe. Seasoning is also meagre. One finds that the Chinese chef will add a little more of the seasonings given. It is very easy to add seasoning, as required, but impossible to remove any excess seasoning added in the first place.

METRIC EQUIVALENTS

It is difficult to convert to French measures with absolute accuracy, but 1 oz. is equal to approximately 30 grammes. 2 lb. 3 oz. to 1 kilogramme.

For liquid measure, approximately 1¾ English pints may be regarded as equal to 1 litre; ½ pint to 3 decilitres (scant); 3½ fluid oz. to 1 decilitre.

OVEN TEMPERATURES

In most recipes in this book reference has been given to the oven temperature or the gas setting. This is an approximate guide only. Different makes of cookers vary and it is a fact that even the same make of cooker can give slightly different individual results at the same temperature or setting.

If in doubt as to whether the temperature given is EXACTLY right for your particular cooker, then do at all times refer to your own manufacturer's temperature chart. It is impossible in a general book to be exact for every cooker, but you will find that the following are a good average in every case.

DESCRIPTION OF OVEN	APPROXIMATE TEMPERATURE CENTRE OF OVEN °F.	THERMOSTAT SETTING
Very Cool	250-275	$\frac{1}{4}-\frac{1}{2}$
Cool	300	1-2
Warm	325	3
Moderate	350	4
Fairly Hot	375-425	5-7
Hot	450	8
Very Hot	475	9

SOLID MEASURE

ENGLISH MEASUREMENTS	APPROXIMATE CONVERSION TABLE	AMERICAN MEASUREMENTS
5 oz.	Almonds, chopped	1 cup
6$\frac{1}{2}$ oz.	Almonds, minced	1 cup
8 oz.	Beef, uncooked	1 cup
8 oz.	Beef, minced	1$\frac{1}{2}$ cups
8 oz.	Chestnuts, chopped	1 cup
8 oz.	Chicken livers, minced	1 cup
8 oz.	Crabmeat	1 cup
4 oz.	Flour	1 cup
6 oz.	Mushrooms, chopped	1$\frac{1}{2}$ cups
3-4 oz.	Mushrooms, button	1 cup
5-6 oz.	Prawns	1 cup
5$\frac{1}{2}$ oz.	Rice, cooked	1 cup
7 oz.	Rice, uncooked	1 cup

CHINESE HOT POT

PIN LO

Pin-Lo is the perfect 'party piece' where the guests themselves participate in the cooking. It is entirely unlike any 'hot pot' we know, Lancashire or other. Indeed, the 'hot pot' is the vessel in which the foods are cooked. The ideal number of guests for the 'feast' is eight to ten and the variety of dishes, as you can see from the photograph on page 14 is quite amazing — but it could be even greater. Ten or eleven different items are a very good selection. As each of them can be bought in small quantities, the cost of a Pin Lo occasion works out much more reasonably than one might think.

People participating in a Pin-Lo meal for the first time will learn in the most practical way one of the chief 'secrets' of the Chinese kitchen — just how very little cooking wafer-thin pieces of fish, meat and poultry need. Each is cooked in the minimum of time — and this applies to vegetables, too.

If, for instance, you have never previously cooked the tender pale green leaves of Savoy or 'ordinary' cabbage in the consommé, you cannot know how delicious and digestible this very often over-cooked (and indigestible) vegetable can be. Have the leaves whole and separate. This means, of course, that you would choose a medium-small rather than large cabbage. Drop the leaves, one at a time, into the boiling consommé and give them just under 5 minutes cooking. They will then be tender, but still crisp, and of a flavour which no cabbage boiled for half an hour could possibly have.

Spinach is another green which could well benefit from being given the minimum of cooking. Choose true spinach, for preference, and the ribs will not be tough. Coarser types such as beet-spinach and the 'perpetual' or New Zealand spinach will need to have their ribs stripped and discarded and their stalks cut off in the same way as you would do for cooking the spinach in the ordinary manner.

Tender spears of sprouting broccoli can also be cooked to advantage for about 6 minutes in the boiling consommé.

While we suggest ten to eleven items in a Pin-Lo party (see below), there is no reason why five to six would not be perfectly satisfactory. The poached eggs (see page 13) could well be omitted since their handling and cooking call for more skill than most people can muster without a little experience.

One dish is 4 oz. or so of very thin strips of fillet steak dressed with beaten egg, pepper, salt, soy sauce and a pinch or two of flour, all well worked into the meat. Another is small pieces of cleaned ink-fish (squid) and a third is a medium-sized Dover sole, filleted and then cut into slender slices. Then there is 4 oz. pig's liver very thinly sliced — not easy unless you know how the Chinese cook does the job. Press one hand on the liver and, with a really sharp knife in the other, very gently cut through into very thin slices. Shelled Pacific prawns, black intestinal lines discarded, are cut into small strips. So is a breast of chicken, skin and nerves removed. On another plate, there is even thinly sliced skinned chicken gizzard, a great delicacy in China. Three to four scallops, white parts only, are cut horizontally into fairly thin slices and are on their own dish ready to be selected and cooked.

Fresh eggs and Chinese pickled ones, the latter bought ready to eat. One simply cracks and removes their outside casing of rice husks and clay, quarters the eggs and places them ready with a garnish of Chinese pickles (see page 140). There are always at

least two kinds of greens. In the present instance, watercress and lettuce. Finally, and very important, there are always three or four sauces from chilli, mustard, onion, and ginger, plum and soy. These sauces are arranged around a pot a little more than half filled with boiling rich chicken stock, resting on a lighted spirit lamp. Guests dip their cooked items in the chosen sauce.

Chopsticks should be used but, for those who cannot manage them, or will not make the effort, long forks can stand in.

The procedure is this:

Each person picks up with chopsticks (or impales on a fork) an item which appeals to him or her — fish, shellfish, meat or greens — drops or lowers it into the just boiling stock and leaves it there just long enough to be cooked. This is a very short time indeed. Most people, at first, leave it longer than necessary but, very soon, a minute or even less will be allowed for each item. Once you have given scallops this quick treatment, it is hardly likely that

you will again resort to even the short time we generally allow this delicious but much neglected bivalve.

The garnishes, as you can see, are simple — onion 'flowers', sprays of parsley and quartered tomatoes.

TO MAKE ONION 'FLOWERS'

Cut four 1½- to 2-inch lengths of firm green spring onion stalks, then cut down one-third way from each end.

Drop them into cold iced water and the ends will spring out into circular fringes or 'flowers'.

So far, the guests have cooked their own items, but, when the time comes for the fresh eggs and lettuce leaves, the host or hostess takes over. The lettuce leaves are carefully arranged in the stock to support the eggs, cup-wise. A raw egg is broken into each 'cup' and poached to individual tastes.

Lastly, when all the items have been consumed, there still remains the lovely broth. Believe it or not, that glorious conglomeration of flavours is the most delicious you will ever come across!

Pin Lo

MENUS

CHAN DAN

The Menus we have suggested here are those we would choose in our favourite Chinese Restaurant, Fu Tong. The dishes 'go together' as it were. But anyone can make just as suitable selections.

As in any other menu planning, one would avoid having two similar important dishes at the one meal.

Further, one would be unlikely to serve two pork dishes at the one meal though, strangely enough, two chicken dishes can appear.

With a few exceptions, such as fried sea bass (see page 51) and Cantonese duck (see page 68), most of the dishes in this book are for two to four persons - mainly two to three persons. This is because when so many dishes are placed on the table at one time, very little of each will suffice. One dish, therefore, which, in our Western way or eating, would serve only two persons can well serve four.

If, however, one prefers to limit the dishes to two with, perhaps, boiled or fried rice, it is very easy to double or even quadruple the various amounts of ingredients given in a dish.

A CELEBRATION MEAL

Pin lo

Candied banana fritters

Jasmine tea

Egg drop soup
Sweet sour pork
Steamed chicken with vegetable garnish
Crispy noodles with chicken and bean sprouts
Lobster balls
Fried rice

Pork and awabi soup
Butterfly prawns
Crispy noodles, pork and bean sprouts
Fried sliced steak
Fried rice with vegetables

Sweet corn and chicken soup
Pacific prawns and black soya bean
Boned duck Cantonese style
Fried soft noodles

Chicken and bamboo shoot soup
Sea bass with sweet sour sauce
Steamed chicken with vegetable garnish
Fried bamboo shoots with water chestnuts
and Chinese mushrooms
Plain boiled rice

Fried Pacific prawns in shells
Barbequed spare ribs
Chicken with white button mushrooms
Fried bamboo shoots with water chestnuts
and Chinese mushrooms
Boiled rice

Pancake rolls sliced
Steamed halibut with vegetables
Chicken livers with cashew nuts
Quick stir lettuce
Fried rice

Roast belly of pork and salad
Chicken with almonds
Crawfish with mixed vegetables
Fried rice with egg

Fried prawns with transparent noodles
Chicken with bean sprouts and crispy noodles
Rump steak and cos lettuce
Stuffed cucumber

Sweet and sour trout
Chicken with oyster sauce
Lobster balls
Escallopes of rump steak and sweet sour sauce
Fried rice

Chicken with bean sprouts
Awabi and Chinese mushrooms
Sweet and sour trout
Pork meat balls
Crispy noodles with chicken and vegetables

Eggs in sweet sour sauce
Fried prawns and pork fat
Rump steak with bean sprouts
Stuffed cucumber
Boiled rice

Paper-wrapped prawns, deep fat fried
Crab creamed with bamboo shoots
Chicken with sweet sour sauce
Fried Brussels sprouts
Boiled rice

Chicken, ham, bamboo shoots and mushrooms
omelet
Chicken with asparagus
Fried bass with vegetable garnish
Bean sprouts and mixed vegetables
Fried rice

Prawns with long life noodles
Duck with almonds
Mushrooms in white sauce
Rice noodles with prawns and chicken

Prawns, egg coated and fried
Barbequed pork and sweet sour sauce
Rice sticks with beef
Chicken with bean sprouts and crispy noodles
Fried spinach

Sweet sour sea bass
Steamed meat in noodle cases
Chicken with peas
Fried spinach
Boiled rice

Chicken prawn and ham omelet
Sweet sour chicken
Stuffed sweet green peppers
Julienne of vegetables
Boiled rice

Crab omelet
Chicken with asparagus
Noodles with mixed meats, prawns and vegetables
Lobster balls
Spring greens

Cut roast belly of pork served with salad
Creamed crab with bamboo shoots
Fillet steak with mixed vegetables, chicken and green peas
Duck with pineapple
Fried rice and vegetables

Almond omelet
Chicken breasts with bean sprouts
Celery in cream sauce
Meat and vegetable with transparent noodles
Fried rice

3. **Sam See Tong.**
Soup with shredded chicken pork etc

91. **Hung Yen Gai Dang**
Stewed chicken with almonds in gravy

20. **Fu-Tong Tick Chow Fan.**
Fu-Tong special rice

99. **Cham Shiu Gai**
sliced chinese roast chicken

77. **Char Har Kow.**
Scampi fritters

121. **Chow Chop Choy**
Bamboo shoots with chinese mushrooms

Hong Shui Pai Guat
Barbecued spare ribs

A Chinese menu card

Butterfly prawns and prawn crackers; barbecued spare ribs; pork pellets; 'water-lily' platter

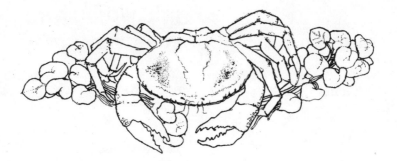

APPETIZERS AND SOUPS

DIM SUM; TONG

The course known to the Western world as *hors-d'oeuvre* is, on a Chinese menu, called *appetizers*. While there are only a few appetizers in this section, other dishes in this book can be served in small portions at this course.

Generally, however, two appetizers should be ample although there is no reason why one should not serve more.

The excellence of Chinese soups is due to the clear stock and the fresh flavour of the added ingredients, which is achieved by the speed at which they are cooked. No vegetables in any of the soups in this book require more than a few minutes cooking. In soups as well as other savoury dishes, the Chinese cook uses Ve-Tsin (M.S.G.) under one or other proprietary name (see page 151). This substance, salt-like in appearance, has the virtue of bringing out and accentuating the flavour of any foods with which it is employed.

In Chinese homes, where chicken figures frequently,

chicken stock is, logically, used for soups. But thrifty cooks buy giblets, whenever possible, and, at the same time, ask for the feet in which there is more goodness than one might think. Chicken gizzards, hearts, skinned feet and necks make beautifully clear stock. Chicken livers, which are part of the giblets one buys, are never used in the stock but are reserved for inclusion in special dishes. I buy chicken giblets from my poulterer-butcher because many people buy chicken without the giblets as they cannot be bothered to do anything with the latter! Another source is where spit-roasted chickens are sold. In each case, the giblets are inexpensive. Beef stock (see page 36) is used in other soups — and the Chinese cook does not disdain chicken and beef bouillon cubes. If you can buy canned clear chicken soup it is first-class. Canned beef consommé is excellent. It saves both time and money because these days the raw material for making clear beef stock is expensive.

FOR TOY CHEN GWAR PIN

HAM AND CUCUMBER SLICES

Preparation time 20-30 minutes
No cooking
To serve 4-5

You will need

1 large cucumber
4 oz. very thin cooked lean ham
plum sauce (bought)
spring onion green

Peel the cucumber. Cut it lengthwise into thin slices

and then into strips approximately 1 inch wide by 2-2½ inches long. Cut the ham into rectangles of similar size and have both cucumber and ham ready. For each ham and cucumber slice, you will need 2 strips of spring onion green. Drop the spring onion green into boiling water and leave them in it (off heat) just long enough to make them pliable. Rinse in cold water, drain and dry. Cut each lengthwise into thin strips and set them aside.

Dot each slice of cucumber with a spot of the plum sauce. Lay a portion of the ham on top and press gently together.

For each 'slice', arrange the ham and cucumber slice on top of the 2 strips of onion green and tie the strips to secure it. Arrange on a serving tray.

PAI GUAT
BARBECUED SPARE RIBS

(Illustrated in colour on page 20)
Preparation time   15-20 minutes
Cooking time   1 hour 10 minutes
To serve   4

You will need

3 onion 'flowers' (see below)
8 spare ribs of pork *
peanut oil
1 tablespoon yellow soya bean (see page 151)
1 tablespoon red bean curd (see page 151)
1 dessertspoon ginger sherry (see page 151)
1 level teaspoon salt
2 tablespoons sugar
1 teaspoon Ve-Tsin (see page 151)
1 tablespoon soy sauce

* Spare ribs, to the Chinese cook, are the end bones of the ribs, 4-5 inches long, with only a little meat on them. To the average butcher, however, they are thick meaty shoulder pieces and they will not do at all for this dish. Butchers who supply Chinese restaurants with meat will know at once what you want if you tell them that the spare ribs are for Chinese cooking.

TO MAKE THE ONION 'FLOWERS'

Cut four 1½- to 2-inch lengths of firm green spring onion stalks, then cut down one-third way from each end.
Drop them into cold iced water and the ends will spring out into circular fringes or 'flowers'.
Allow 2 ribs per person, as above. Wash them well in cold water. Spread a little peanut oil over the inside of a roasting tin or heatproof dish which will hold the ribs comfortably in one row. Lay the spare ribs in it.
In a basin, mix and pound together to a pulp the soya bean and bean curd. Well work in the sherry, salt, sugar and Ve-Tsin to a smooth pulp. Add and work in the soy sauce. Cover the spare ribs with this mixture. Place for 20 minutes in a very hot oven (450°F. or Gas Mark 8). Turn the ribs and give them another 30 minutes, then turn them again and give them 20 minutes more.
Place with their sauce on a heated serving dish and garnish with the onion 'flowers'.

JAR WON TON
PORK PELLETS

(Illustrated in colour on page 20)
Preparation time   25-30 minutes
Cooking time   3-4 minutes
To serve   4

You will need

½ recipe noodle dough (see page 31)
4 onion 'flowers' (see below) or sprigs watercress
2 tablespoons cooked pork
2 tablespoons raw Pacific prawns
1 Chinese mushroom
2 canned water chestnuts
tiny pinch salt
tiny pinch sugar
tiny pinch Ve-Tsin (see page 151)
1 small teaspoon ginger sherry (see page 151)
few drops sesame oil
shake or two pepper
little beaten egg
peanut oil for deep frying

Make the noodle dough and prepare the onion 'flowers' as follows.
Cut four 1½- to 2-inch lengths of firm green spring onion stalks, then cut down one-third way from each end.
Drop them into cold iced water and the ends will spring out into circular fringes or 'flowers'.

Very finely chop the pork, cleaned prawns, mushroom and water chestnuts. Mix them together. Add the next 6 ingredients and work them thoroughly together.
Leave for the time being.
Roll out the noodle dough to about $\frac{1}{16}$ inch thick.
Cut it into 3-inch strips and then 3-inch squares. Place a portion of the filling on one corner of each square and proceed as for pork pellets in the recipe for pork pellet soup on page 34.
Heat the peanut oil in a suitable pan for deep frying. Test with a sliver of raw potato as for prawn crackers (see page 45).
Cook the 'pellets', a few at a time, to a warm golden colour.
Drain on absorbent paper, place in a heated serving dish and garnish with the onion 'flowers' or sprigs of watercress.

CHEN GUIN
PANCAKE ROLLS
(SPRING ROLLS)

Preparation time   10 minutes
Cooking time   7-8 minutes
To serve   4-5

You will need

PANCAKE BATTER

4 oz. plain flour

pinch salt

1 egg

½ pint (U.S. 1¼ cups) water

FILLING

1 level tablespoon each raw pork, ham and
  chicken

1 tablespoon bean sprouts

1 level tablespoon Chinese mushrooms
  (see page 150)

1 level tablespoon canned bamboo shoots

1 dessertspoon peanut oil

1 level tablespoon shrimps

1 finely chopped onion

pinch each salt, sugar and Ve-Tsin
  (see 151 page)

few drops soy sauce

½ teaspoon ginger sherry (see page 151)

sprigs parsley to garnish

TO MAKE THE BATTER

Sift the flour and salt into a basin. Make a well in
the centre. Drop in the egg and gradually stir in
the water to make a very thin batter about the
thickness of thin cream. Set aside for an hour.

TO MAKE THE FILLING

Cut the pork, ham and chicken into thin strips. Pick
over the bean sprouts and discard any empty seed
cases. Cut the stalkless mushrooms and bamboo
shoots into thin slices.
Heat the oil in the frying-pan and cook the onion in
it for ¼ minute. Add the 3 meats and cook for
1 minute. Add the bean sprouts and shrimps and
cook for ¼ minute, then add the mushrooms and
bamboo shoots and cook for ⅓ minute more, tossing
the mixture about.
Add the seasonings, soy sauce and sherry and turn
the mixture about over a reduced heat for not more
than ½ minute to coat it with the flavourings. Leave
to become cold.

TO MAKE THE PANCAKES

Very lightly oil a frying-pan 7-8 inches in diameter, and get it fairly warm. Pour 2 tablespoons

Pancake rolls

of the batter into the pan and turn it this way and
that to coat the bottom. (If the pan is too hot, you
will have a little difficulty in spreading the batter
evenly.)
Raise the heat a little and gently cook the pancake
on one side only. Repeat until all the batter, except
a dessertspoon, has been used. This amount of
batter will make 4-5 pancakes. Lay each pancake,
cooked side down.
When ready to fill them, turn each pancake over.
Place a portion of the filling on one half of each
pancake and bring the other side up and over it.
Brush each of the ends with a little of the batter
reserved for the purpose. Bring them up and over
and very gently press them to form the pancake into
a neat thickish roll.
Have a deep pan half filled with hot peanut oil
(380°F. or 193°C.) To test the heat of the oil drop
a slice of raw potato into it. If the potato slice
immediately bounces up the oil is the correct
temperature. Cook the pancakes till a pale golden
colour. Lift them out and roll on to a piece of
absorbent kitchen paper.
Arrange the pancakes on a heated serving dish and
garnish with parsley.
Note
In spite of what some people believe, there is no
mystique about the making of pancake rolls. All
one has to bear in mind is that they should be
wafer-thin and pliable and are cooked on one side
only.
Further, the filling is placed on the cooked side of
the pancakes before they are rolled up.
The result of cooking pancakes this way is that they
are more attractive as their surfaces are not exactly
smooth.

FUNG MAI HAR AND HAR BENG

BUTTERFLY PRAWNS AND PRAWN CRACKERS

(Illustrated in colour on page 120)
Preparation time   6 minutes
Cooking time   3-4 minutes
To serve   4

You will need

6 raw Pacific prawns
pinch salt
shake pepper
pinch sugar
pinch Ve-Tsin (see page 151)
1 egg
1-2 oz. toasted breadcrumbs
peanut oil
12 prawn crackers (see page 45)

TO PREPARE THE PRAWNS

Shell the prawns, if necessary. Halve each prawn lengthwise and remove the black intestinal lines. Trim off any rough edges but leave the tail ends intact.
Have the breadcrumbs ready on a plate but do not coat the prawns as yet with the seasoned egg and breadcrumbs.

TO FRY THE PRAWN CRACKERS

Place the oil in a deep fryer or thick pot to a depth of about 4 inches. Have a frying basket in it while it heats. Test the temperature by dropping a sliver of raw potato into the oil. If it rests for a few seconds and then rises to the surface, it is ready. If it bounces right up, the oil is too hot and the crackers will not expand into the delightful crisp white tasty morsels they should be but will expand only a little. Drop the crackers into the hot oil and, when they rise, give them 8 seconds. Immediately, lift them out and drain them on absorbent kitchen paper. Coat the prepared prawns in the prepared seasoned egg and breadcrumbs. Lower them into the very hot oil and cook them for about 2 minutes when they will be cooked to a beautifully deep warm gold and curled most attractively. Drain as above.
Place each half prawn in the 'cup' of a prawn cracker and pile them on a serving dish.

Chicken livers and cashew nuts

GAI KUN YU KO

CHICKEN LIVERS AND CASHEW NUTS

Prepdration time   5 minutes
Cooking time   about 8 minutes
To serve   2

You will need

2 chicken livers, cleaned and trimmed
4 canned water chestnuts
4-5 canned bamboo shoots
2-3 slices onion
1½-2 tablespoons peanut oil
pinch each salt, sugar and Ve-Tsin
   (see page 151)
few drops soy sauce
4 tablespoons chicken stock
½ teaspoon cornflour
1 tablespoon water
3-4 tablespoons roasted salt cashew nuts
parsley

Drop the livers into salted boiling water and cook for 3-4 minutes. Drain; leave to become cold. Then slice livers, water chestnuts and bamboo shoots. Heat peanut oil in a frying-pan. Add onion and fry for 1 minute. Add liver and fry and toss onion and liver about for 1 minute. Add water chestnuts and bamboo shoots and cook for 1 minute more. Add salt, sugar, Ve-Tsin and soy sauce and chicken stock and toss all about. Blend the cornflour in the water and add it to the vegetable mixture. Boil up and let simmer for

1½ minutes. Finally add the roasted cashew nuts and heat them through. Turn everything into a heated serving dish and garnish with parsley.

GOH BAR HAR
PRAWNS
WITH CRISPY FRIED RICE

Preparation time   3-4 hours
Cooking time   about 8-9 minutes
To serve   2-3

You will need

3-4 Pacific prawns
1 tablespoon dry white wine
pinch each salt and pepper
1 crushed clove garlic
1-2 tablespons tubed tomato purée
water
½ tablespoon cornflour
peanut oil
3-4 oz. prepared rice *

* The Chinese never waste anything, and in this recipe the rice is that which is left in the bottom of the pot when rice is boiled. It is dried and then scraped off in as large layers as possible. The rice is dried out in a cool oven and slightly resembles Melba toast in that one side is golden and smooth and the other slightly rough and hardly coloured.

Shell, clean and cut the prawns into 1-inch pieces. Work the white wine, salt and pepper into them, and if used, the crushed clove of garlic. Then discard the latter.
Blend together the tomato purée and 2-3 tablespoons water and bring to the boil. Blend the cornflour and 1 dessertspoon water and stir into the tomato mixture. Boil for 1½ minutes.
Heat 1 tablespoon of peanut oil in frying-pan. Turn the prepared prawns into it and cook, tossing and turning them for 3-4 minutes. Turn them into the sauce. Meanwhile heat till very hot enough peanut oil for deep frying. Turn the prepared rice into it. The oil should be so hot that the rice immediately rises to the surface and browns very quickly. Have ready 2 bowls, one larger than the other and one very hot. Turn the prawns in their sauce into the smaller one and the rice, straight from the hot oil and quickly drained, into the other. Take them to the table immediately, and at once turn the prawns and sauce into the rice.

Preserved Chinese eggs

PEI DAN
PRESERVED CHINESE EGGS

Chinese preserved eggs, as shown in the above photograph, have a thick coating of rice husks and clay. This coating is cracked and carefully removed. Serve the eggs as required.
The photograph below shows the preserved eggs, cut lengthwise in quarters and garnished with sliced ginger and Chinese pickles (see page 140). Preserved Chinese eggs are often served as appetizers.

Preserved Chinese eggs

YEUNG MOW GOO
STUFFED MUSHROOMS

Preparation time   20 minutes
Cooking time   9-10 minutes
To serve   3

You will need

6 open mushrooms *
2 oz. raw pork, including a little fat
2 thin slices canned bamboo shoots
3 canned water chestnuts
1 rounded teaspoon chopped onion
1 teaspoon chicken stock
pinch each salt and Ve-Tsin (see page 151)
1 teaspoon soy sauce
1 rounded teaspoon cornflour
1 teaspoon water
2-3 tablespoons peanut oil
2 onion 'flowers' (see page 22)

* The mushrooms should be $1\frac{1}{2}$-$1\frac{3}{4}$ inches in diameter.

After removing the stems, float the mushrooms, gill sides down, in a bowl of cold water and tap them to remove any sand. Wipe the tips and drain the mushrooms, gill sides down. Chop the pork. (The Chinese use two knives, one in each hand.) Add the bamboo shoots and water chestnuts and chop all very finely. Add the onion, chicken stock, seasonings and soy sauce and, finally, the cornflour, blended with the water. Beat this 'dough', time and again, on the table until firm.

Stuffed mushroms

Divide into 6 equal portions and pack one firmly into each mushroom. Set aside.

Turn the oil into a frying-pan large enough to contain the 6 mushrooms in one layer. Get the oil fairly hot. Gently lower the mushrooms, stuffed sides down, into it and cook for 1 minute. Reduce the heat and cook for another 4-5 minutes. Turn the mushrooms and cook the tops for 2 minutes. Drain, place on a heated serving dish and garnish with the onion 'flowers'.

TUNG FOON
'WATER-LILY' PLATTER

(Illustrated in colour on page 20)
Preparation time   15-20 minutes
No cooking
To serve   4

You will need

canned bamboo shoots
unpeeled cucumber
'water-lily' radishes (see below)
4-6 wafer thin slices cooked duck
4-5 wafer thin slices lean ham
4-6 wafer thin slices white
   chicken meat
4-6 wafer thin slices canned awabi
6 mushrooms
canned green asparagus

Slice the bamboo shoots and the unpeeled cucumber to your liking. Prepare the 'water-lily' radishes (see below). Fold the slices of cooked duck, ham, chicken meat and awabi and arrange the various ingredients to make an attractive pattern (see colour photograph on page 20). This arrangement also enables the guests to help themselves to what they like, without disturbing the arrangement too much. Group each ingredient for colour contrast. For instance, the green asparagus separating the white chicken meat; the green cucumber accenting the bamboo shoots and so on.

The centre-piece is awabi cut into petal shapes to form a flower.

TO MAKE RADISH 'WATER-LILIES'

Choose radishes of good shape. See that they are not too long and not too squat. Starting at the pointed end of each radish, cut petal shapes almost to the base with a small sharp knife.

Drop the radishes into very cold, preferably iced, water and the 'petals' will spring out.

FONG WONG KHIN
PHOENIX ROLL

(Illustrated in colour on page 58)

Preparation time   about 10 minutes
Cooking time   30 minutes
To serve   3-4

You will need

1 teaspoon peanut oil
pancake mixture (see page 23)

FILLING

6 oz. raw pork ($\frac{3}{4}$ of it fat)
1 dessertspoon canned water chestnuts
1 dessertspoon canned bamboo shoots
$\frac{1}{2}$ Chinese mushroom (see page 150)
1 dessertspoon shelled cooked prawns
pinch each salt, sugar and Ve-Tsin
   (see page 151)
few drops soy sauce
1 teaspoon beaten whole egg
1 thin strip boiled ham (5 inches $\times$ $\frac{1}{4}$ inch)
2 strips bamboo shoots (3 inches long, $\frac{3}{4}$ inch
   square)
peanut oil for deep frying

TO MAKE THE PANCAKE

Very gently warm the peanut oil in a large frying-pan. The pancake must remain yellow, so the oil must not be hot. Pour in enough pancake mixture to make the thinnest possible layer, cook until just firm then remove to a lightly oiled surface.

TO MAKE THE FILLING

Finely chop the pork, the water chestnuts, the bamboo shoots, the mushroom and the cooked prawns. Add the salt, sugar, Ve-Tsin and soy sauce. Beat well together, throwing the mixture on the table time and again to combine the ingredients very well.

Form into an oblong about 5$\frac{1}{2}$ inches by 2$\frac{1}{2}$ inches. Sprinkle very little beaten egg over the pancake and smooth it over evenly with the finger tips. Place the oblong on the side of the pancake nearest you, about 3 inches back from the edge. Arrange the strip of ham down the centre of the mixture with a strip of bamboo shoot on either side of it. Bring the far side of the pancake over the filling then bring each side up and over and press gently together. Trickle a little more beaten egg on the surfaces which have none on them. Beginning with the side nearest you, roll up the pancake into a thickish sausage-like shape with the ends tucked in.

Steam for 20 minutes. Drain well; drop into medium hot oil and cook for 8—10 minutes until golden brown.

SAM SEE TONG
CHICKEN
AND BAMBOO SHOOTS

(Illustrated in colour on page 36)

Preparation time   5-6 minutes
Cooking time   4 minutes
To serve   4

You will need

3 oz. raw chicken breast
2 oz. boiled ham
2 oz. canned bamboo shoots
1-2 oz. cultivated mushrooms
1-2 springs onions, if available
1$\frac{1}{2}$ pints (U.S. 3$\frac{3}{4}$ cups) chicken stock or
   1 chicken bouillon cube and water
1 dessertpoon peanut oil
pinch salt
$\frac{1}{4}$ teaspoon sugar
pinch Ve-Tsin (see page 151)
few drops ginger sherry (see below)

Cut the chicken breast into thin strips and set them aside. Cut the boiled ham and bamboo shoots into similar strips and place them together in another dish.

Slice the mushrooms very thinly and on the bias cut the onions, if used, into 1-inch pieces. Heat the chicken stock or the chicken bouillon with water. Heat the peanut oil in a frying-pan and quickly cook the chicken strips in it for a minute, tossing and turning them, without colouring them.

Add the ham, bamboo shoots and mushrooms and cook them a further minute. Add to the chicken stock the onions, if used, the salt, sugar and Ve-Tsin. Cook 1 minute.

Add the prepared meats and vegetables and bring to the boil. Add the ginger sherry.

GINGER SHERRY

One makes one's own with green ginger, available at any Chinese emporium.

Chop $\frac{1}{2}$-1 oz. green ginger or cut it into thin strips. Place in a bottle which will hold $\frac{2}{5}$ pint (U.S. 1 cup) liquid and fill up with inexpensive brown, not-too-sweet sherry.

Leave to infuse for a few days.

GUM LO GEE LEE

SPICED PIG'S TONGUE

Preparation time   5 minutes
Cooking time   up to 40 minutes
To serve   3

You will need

1 pig's tongue (fresh)
3-4 tablespoons soy sauce
1 teaspoon sugar
pinch salt
½ teaspoon ginger sherry (see page 27)
little pepper
6 tablespoons water

Well wash and drain the tongue and have it ready.
Blend together the remaining ingredients and bring
them to the boil in a pan into which the tongue will
fit closely enough for the marinade (liquid) to cover
it. Leave to become cold.
Add the tongue; slowly bring the liquid to the
boil then simmer very gently until the tongue is
tender.
Skin it while it is fairly hot and leave it to become
cold.
Place the tongue on a cutting board. Place one hand
flat on it and, with a sharp knife in the other, cut
it into the thinnest possible slices diagonally or, as
we might say, on the bias.
Arrange the slices in rows on a serving-dish. Serve
without any sauce.

HAR DOR SEE

PRAWN PASTE FRITTER

Preparation time   10-12 minutes
Cooking time   4-5 minutes
To serve   2-3

You will need

3 prawns, shelled and cleaned
tiny pinch Ve-Tsin (see page 151)
pinch pepper
3 large extremely thin slices bread
1 large egg white
pinch salt
1 small tablespoon very finely chopped lean
    cooked ham

Very finely mince the prawns and pound into a
paste with a potato masher or wooden spoon.
Add the Ve-Tsin and pepper.
Trim the crust from the bread and cut each slice
each into three two-finger widths. (If the slices
are small you can use four or five slices of
bread.) Whip the egg white to meringue stage
with a pinch of salt and gently fold it into the
prawns so that the meringue remains firm in
texture. Divide this mixture evenly between the
slices of bread moulding each portion lightly but
firmly to the bread, and at the same time leaving
a nice rounded surface. Tidy the edges. In a frying-
pan large enough, if possible, to take all these at
once, put about ¼ inch deep peanut oil. Heat it
fairly hot and place the bread in it. Baste the oil
over the egg white. When the bread is golden and
the egg white firm, but not brown, it is cooked. Lift
out and drain. Sprinkle the centre of each with the
finely chopped ham and serve.

GUM LO JUN GON

SPICED GIBLETS

Preparation time   8-10 minutes
Cooking time   40-50 minutes
To serve   4

You will need

4 chicken or duck gizzards
2 chicken or duck livers
3-4 tablespoons soy sauce
1 teaspoon sugar
1 teaspoon ginger sherry (see page 27)
6 tablespoons water

After removing the 'bags', well wash the gizzards
and put them aside. Wash the livers, too.
Make a marinade by bringing the soy sauce, sugar,
sherry and water to the boil in a small pan.
Leave to become cold. Add the gizzards and livers.
Cover and bring slowly to the boil. Simmer for
15-20 minutes, then remove the livers and leave
them to become cold. Continue to simmer until the
gizzards are cooked. Remove them and leave them
to become cold.
Trim the tough skin off the gizzards, then very
thinly slice them and the livers. Serve cold without
any sauce.

TO SERVE HOT

Reheat the slices in the marinade and serve a little
of it as 'sauce'.

JAR HAR JAI

SHRIMPS IN BATTER

Preparation time   a few minutes
Cooking time   2-3 minutes
To serve   2-3

You will need

4-oz. packet frozen Norwegian cooked
   prawns *
4 oz. self-raising flour
pinch flour
salt
$\frac{1}{4}$ pint (U.S. $\frac{2}{3}$ cup) water
peanut oil
washed and dried lettuce leaves

* The 'shrimps' here are actually Norwegian
prawns. In the United States these are shrimps.

Defrost and drain the prawns and have them ready.
Sift the flour and salt into a basin. Stir in the water.
Leave to rest for an hour in order to disperse any
elasticity introduced to the batter by stirring. Have
a pan half filled with the oil. Heat it to 375°—380°F.
or 190°—193°C. Dip the prawns in the batter and
drain off excess. Drop them into the hot oil and
cook until golden in colour. Lift out with a wire
skimmer, place a portion on 2—3 lettuce leaves
and serve.

KWAI FAR CHI

SHARK'S FIN OMELET

Preparation time   overnight
Cooking time   3-4 hours
To serve   2-3

You will need

Shark's fin, bought already prepared
hot chicken stock
3 tablespoon bean sprouts (see page 102)
2-3 eggs
peanut oil
pinch salt
tiny pinch pepper

Well cover the shark's fin with cold water and leave
to soak all night. Next day drain and wash thoroughly. Cover with stock and let simmer for 3-4
hours. Drain and shred it. Meanwhile pick over,
wash and rinse the bean sprouts. To make the
omelet, beat the eggs together just enough to blend
them. Heat $1\frac{1}{2}$ tablespoons peanut oil.
Very gently cook shark fin, without colouring, for
1 minute. Add bean sprouts, cook for $\frac{1}{2}$ minute. To
eggs work in the salt, pepper and $\frac{1}{2}$ coffee spoon
peanut oil. Pour over shark's fin mixture. Toss
and turn mixture not allowing to colour.
When just ready to come together, form into an
oval cushion shape and turn on to a warm serving
dish.
The Chinese omelet is a mixture of ingredients held
together with the beaten egg. It should be succulent,
moist but not 'runny' inside, and never firm.

HAI YUK SUN TONG

ASPARAGUS
AND CRAB VELOUTE

Preparation time   3-4 minutes
Cooking time   4-5 minutes
To serve   3-4

You will need

8 canned asparagus tips
1 oz. white crab meat (canned or frozen)
$1\frac{1}{2}$ pints (U.S. $3\frac{3}{4}$ cups) rich chicken stock
pinch Ve-Tsin, if required (see page 151)
salt and pepper, if required
1 small teaspoon cornflour
1 tablespon water
1 egg white

Cut the asparagus tips into pea-sized pieces. Flake
the crab meat. Have the asparagus and the crab
meat ready. Heat the chicken stock. If not rich
enough, add a pinch of Ve-Tsin. Taste and season
further, if necessary. Add the asparagus and crab
meat.
Blend the cornflour with the water and stir it into
the soup. Boil for 2 minutes. Remove from the heat
and add the slightly beaten egg white, whisking
vigorously.
Serve at once.

Note

A very pleasant asparagus and chicken soup can be
made in the same way.
Substitute 3-4 tablespoons of chopped chicken
from white cut chicken (see page 61) for the crab
meat.

CHUNG KWOK SANG

CHINESE SALAD

Preparation time   20 minutes
Cooking time   12-13 minutes
To serve   2-3

You will need

1 large Chinese mushroom soaked 1 hour
   (see page 150)
little chicken stock
3-4 tablespoons bean sprouts
3 tablespoons peanut oil
1 tablespoon white wine vinegar
1 teaspoon soy sauce
4 oz. poached chicken, cut into strips *
½ fair-sized lettuce, cut into strips
salt and pepper to taste

* The chicken will have more flavour if it is poached
originally in chicken stock.

Have each of the ingredients ready. Rinse the
soaked mushroom; cover with chicken stock and
then cook for 10 minutes. Drain the mushroom and
cut it into thin strips and leave to become cold.
Pick over the bean sprouts removing any little seed
shells. Wash and rinse and cook in a little chicken
stock for 2-3 minutes. Drain and leave to become
cold. Blend the peanut oil, vinegar and soy sauce
together. Dress the chicken and lettuce with the oil
and vinegar dressing and serve.

HAI KIM

CRAB CLAWS

Preparation time   10-12 minutes
Cooking time   4 minutes
To serve   2-4

You will need

4 cooked crab claws
2-3 cooked Pacific prawns
pinch pepper
pinch salt
pinch sugar
pinch Ve-Tsin (see page 151)
egg white
peanut oil
1 teaspoon cornflour

Very carefully crack the crab claws without dam-
aging the nipper ends and remove the shells, leaving
each claw meat intact. Shell the prawns and remove
the black intestinal lines.
Chop the prawn meat to pulp. Add the seasonings
and just enough beaten egg white to bind the
mixture. Divide into four portions and mould each
to the meat from one claw, leaving the nipper end
free.
Allow to rest while the oil is being heated.
Dip the crab pieces in the cornflour, then deep-fat
fry them at 375°F. or 190°C. until the surfaces are
golden toned.
Serve at once.

YAU PAU KON PUI

SCALLOPS SHANGHAIENNES

Preparation time   8-10 minutes
Cooking time   4-5 minutes
To serve   2-3

You will need

4-6 scallops
3 canned water chestnuts, sliced
2 tablespoons green peppers, in strips
salt and pepper to taste
1-2 tablespoons peanut oil
1 tablespoon sliced canned bamboo shoots
3 small thinly sliced champignons de Paris
2-3 tablespoons chicken stock
½ teaspoon soy sauce
1 dessertspoon cornflour
1 dessertspoon water

Trim off hard substance around white part of scallops and cut across the grain in thin slices and set
aside.
Place aside water chestnuts and green peppers
cut into small diamonds. Lightly season everything.
Heat 1 tablespoon peanut oil and in it cook for
1 minute the peppers; add bamboo shoots and
cook for ½ minute; add mushrooms and cook for
1 minute. Turn on to a hot plate. Add remaining
oil to pan. Turn sliced scallops into pan and cook
for 1 minute, tossing and turning them continuously. Add vegetables to scallops. Add hot
stock, and soy sauce. Blend cornflour and water,
and add it. Cook for 1 minute; turn into a hot dish
and serve.

SAM SIK LAIN PUN
TRI COLOUR PLATTER

Preparation time   overnight plus 10 minutes
Cooking time   30 minutes
To serve   4-5

You will need

1 breast from 2¾-3 lb. chicken
4 Chinese mushrooms soaked 1 hour, stalks
   discarded (see page 150) *
2 tablespoons peanut oil
2 thin slices fresh ginger, chopped
1 tablespoon soy sauce
1 dessertspoon sugar
6 oz. boiled ham, in one piece

Fairly generously sprinkle the breast of the chicken all over with salt. Leave overnight and next morning wash off the salt. Place on a plate on a steamer and steam for 30 minutes. Remove the chicken from the steamer and leave to become cold. Drain and rinse the mushrooms. Heat the peanut oil in a frying-pan, add the chopped fresh ginger slices and the mushrooms, the soy sauce and sugar. Very gently cook them together taking great care not to burn the mushrooms. When all the sauce, oil and sugar have been absorbed by the mushrooms, remove them from the heat and leave them to become cold.

To assemble the platter, place the chicken breasts flat on to the cutting board and with a very sharp knife cut wafer thin slices slant-wise, and arrange them on the platter in a semi-circle and overlapping each other.

Then cut the mushrooms in a similar manner and arrange them overlapping each other inside the semi-circle of chicken slices.

Thinly slice the ham and arrange the slices overlapping each other and inside the curve of the mushrooms.

DAN MIN
NOODLE DOUGH

Preparation time   up to 15 minutes
Cooking time   as given in the respective
                      recipes

You will need

6 oz. plain flour
1 egg
1 dessertspoon peanut oil
little water

Turn the flour on to an enamel tray or enamel-topped table and make a well in it, deep enough for the remaining ingredients. Drop in the egg, the oil and the water. Begin to mix together with the tip of a finger, bringing the flour in circles into the centre. As you do this, you may find that a little more water is required but be very sparing with it. When the ingredients have been thoroughly combined, work them together to a smooth dough.

Using the heel of the hand, knead the dough out a little and fold it over and over until it is really pliable. Place it in a plastic bag and leave it to rest for a little.

The dough is now ready to be rolled out. Cut as required for any dish in which it is needed.

Incidentally, there is a domestic machine which rolls out the dough and cuts it into thin noodles or, if wanted, strips wide enough for the pork pellets in the soup on page 34.

GAI YUNG SUK MAI TONG
SWEET CORN
AND CHICKEN SOUP

(Illustrated in colour on page 37)
Preparation time   6-7 minutes
Cooking time   about 3 minutes
To serve   4

You will need

4 tablespoons raw chicken
1 large egg white
1½ pints (U.S. 3¾ cups) chicken broth
   or 1 chicken bouillon cube and water
4 tablespoons sweet corn
pinch salt
pinch Ve-Tsin (see page 151)
few drops sesame oil
1 level teaspoon cornflour
1 tablespoon water
2 tablespoons finely chopped cooked ham

Mince the chicken very finely. Beat the egg white just enough to mix the 'thick' with the 'thin'. Thourouhly work it and the chicken together and set aside.

To the broth add the sweet corn and bring to the boil. Add the salt, Ve-Tsin and sesame oil. Stir in the cornflour mixed with the water and boil for 1 minute.

Add the prepared chicken and egg white and boil for a further minute, stirring all the time.

Finally, sprinkle the ham on top and serve.

DAN FAR TONG
EGG DROP SOUP

(Illustrated in colour on page 37)

Preparation time   7-8 minutes
Cooking time   4 minutes
To serve   4

You will need

3 oz. canned bamboo shoots
2 small cultivated mushrooms
1½ oz. cooked peas
2 sliced skinned small tomatoes
3 oz. roast chicken (white meat only)
2 eggs
1½ pints (U.S. 3¾ cups) chicken stock or
   1 chicken bouillon cube and water
pinch salt
pinch sugar
pinch Ve-Tsin (see page 151)
few drops sesame oil
few drops ginger sherry (see page 151)

Cut the bamboo shoots into strips and the mushrooms into very thin slices. Add the peas, tomatoes and thinly sliced chicken. Beat the eggs and leave aside.

Bring the chicken stock to the boil. Add the prepared ingredients except the eggs and cook for 1-2 minutes. Add the salt, sugar, Ve-Tsin, sesame oil and ginger sherry and cook for ½ minute.

Trickle the beaten eggs into the soup, stirring as you do so. Cook for ¼ minute, then serve at once.

BOW YU YUK TONG
PORK AND AWABI SOUP

Preparation time   4-5 minutes
Cooking time   6 minutes
To serve   4

You will need

4 green onion 'flowers' (see page 41), optional
2½ oz. lean pork
2 oz. canned awabi
1½ oz. canned bamboo shoots
1½ pints (U.S. 3¾ cups) chicken stock or
   1 chicken bouillon cube and water
pinch salt
pinch sugar
pinch Ve-Tsin (see page 151)

Cut the raw pork into very thin slices and place

Pork and awabi soup

them in a dish by themselves. Cut the awabi into very thin slices and the bamboo shoots into thin strips. Place them together in another dish. Bring the stock to the boil. Drop the pork into it and cook for 5 minutes. Add the awabi, bamboo shoots and remaining ingredients and boil gently for 1 minute. Meanwhile, shake the water from the onion 'flowers'. Turn the soup into a heated tureen and garnish it with the 'flowers'.

Note

When making this or any other soup, always spoon off any froth that rises.

GAI SEE MIN TONG
CHICKEN NOODLE SOUP

Preparation time   3-4 minutes
Cooking time   10 minutes
To serve   4

You will need

2-3 oz. fine egg noodles (see page 150)
boiling salted water
2-3 oz. cooked white chicken meat
1½ oz. canned bamboo shoots
1 dessertspoon shredded 'hot' Chinese
   cabbage (see page 79)
1½ pints (U.S. 3¾ cups) chicken stock or
   1 chicken bouillon cube and water
pinch salt
pinch Ve-Tsin (see page 151)

Drop the noodles into very slightly salted boiling water and leave to cook for 6-8 minutes.

Chicken noodle soup

Chicken and mushroom soup

Meanwhile, cut the chicken and bamboo shoots into strips. Place them ready with the Chinese cabbage.

Bring the stock to the boil. Drain the noodles, rinse them and drain them again. Add them to the stock, together with the chicken, bamboo shoots and cabbage. Boil up for 2-3 minutes. Season lightly with salt and Ve-Tsin, remembering that the stock, noodles and cabbage already have salt in them.

MOW GOO GAI PIN TONG
CHICKEN AND MUSHROOM SOUP

Preparation time   10 minutes
Cooking time   5 minutes
To serve   4

You will need

4 oz. raw chicken breast
2 oz. cultivated mushrooms
3 oz. canned bamboo shoots
1½ pints (U.S. 3¾ cups) chicken stock or
  1 chicken bouillon cube and water
pinch salt
pinch Ve-Tsin (see page 151)

Cut the chicken into small haricot bean-sized pieces. Slice the mushrooms and the bamboo shoots. Keep all three separate. Bring the stock to the boil. Drop the chicken into it and cook for 4 minutes. Add mushrooms and cook for ½ minute, then add bamboo shoots and cook together for a further ½ minute. Add seasonings and serve.

SUN LARD TONG
PEKIN SOUR AND HOT SOUP

Preparation time   overnight for soaking lichen,
                     plus 8 minutes
Cooking time   35-40 minutes
To serve   4

You will need

4-6 pieces lichen *
1 Chinese mushroom (see page 150)
1¾-2 pints (U.S. 4¼-5 cups) chicken stock
4 tablespoons raw ham, pork or raw chicken,
  cut into thin strips
2 tablespoons canned bamboo shoots
salt and white pepper
white wine vinegar
1 teaspoon cornflour
1 tablespoon water
1 egg
* Lichen is expensive and could be omitted.

Soak the lichen (MOK YE) overnight in cold water and cut into not too small slices. Soak the mushroom, stem discarded, for 1 hour, and slice into suitable pieces. Bring the stock to the boil; add the pork or chicken and let simmer 2 minutes. Then add the bamboo shoots. Add a little salt and generous amount of pepper and the vinegar. Cover and let simmer for 30 minutes. Blend the cornflour and water, stir into the saucepan and let simmer 1½ minutes. Remove from heat and trickle the beaten egg in whilst stirring and serve.

Pork pellet soup

WON TON

PORK PELLET SOUP

Preparation time　25 minutes
Cooking time　　　10 minutes
To serve　　　　　4

You will need

PELLETS

¼ recipe noodle dough (see page 31)
1½ tablespoons roast pork
1 tablespoon canned bamboo shoots
1 Chinese mushroom (see page 150)
1 canned water chestnut
tiny pinch each salt, sugar and Ve-Tsin
　(see page 151)
egg white

SOUP

1½ pints (U.S. 3¾ cups) chicken stock
1 thinly sliced Chinese mushroom
1 thinly sliced canned water chestnut
1½ oz. thinly sliced canned bamboo shoots
3 oz. thinly shredded spring cabbage
pinch salt
pinch Ve-Tsin
4 onion 'flowers' (see page 41)

TO MAKE THE PORK PELLETS

Make the noodle dough as directed, place it in
a plastic bag and leave it for up to an hour. Chop
the pork, bamboo shoots, mushrooms and water
chestnut. Mix them together and season with the

salt, sugar and Ve-Tsin. Roll out the dough to
$\frac{1}{16}$ inch thick and cut it into a strip 3 inches wide
and again into 3-inch squares. Divide the filling
between them. Place a portion firmly on one corner
of each square. Fold over in a narrow fold and fold
again. Dot one side with beaten egg and bring
the opposite side over and under and pinch
together.

TO MAKE THE SOUP

Bring the stock to the boil while preparing the
vegetables for the soup. Drop the pork pellet
'packages' into the stock and cook them for
8 minutes. Add the vegetables and seasoning and
boil for a further 2-3 minutes. Garnish the soup
with the onion 'flowers'.

Note

If the noodle dough is not really thin (about $\frac{1}{16}$
inch), the 'packages' will require a little longer
cooking.

HAI YONG SHOK MEI TONG

SWEET CORN AND CRAB SOUP

Preparation time　4-5 minutes
Cooking time　　　3-4 minutes
To serve　　　　　4

You will need

3 oz. cooked or canned white crab meat
1 large egg white
1½ pints (U.S. 3¾ cups) chicken stock or
　1 chicken bouillon cube and water
2½-3 oz. sweet corn
pinch salt
pinch Ve-Tsin
few drops sesame oil
1 teaspoon ginger sherry (see page 151)
1 level teaspoon cornflour
1 tablespoon water

Very finely shred the crab meat. Beat the egg white
to blend the 'thick' with the 'thin'. Add it to the
crab meat, work it in thoroughly and set aside.
Bring the chicken stock to the boil. Add the sweet
corn to the stock and bring to the boil again. Add
the salt, Ve-Tsin, sesame oil and ginger sherry.
Blend the cornflour with the water, add it to the
stock and boil for ½ minute.
Finally add the crab meat and egg white mixture;
bring to the boil for ¼ minute and serve.

Sweet corn and crab soup

Beef and vegetable soup

NGOW YUK CHOY TONG
BEEF AND VEGETABLE SOUP

Preparation time   6-7 minutes
Cooking time   6-7 minutes
To serve   4

You will need

4 green onion 'flowers' (see page 41)
3-4 oz. raw rump steak
1 tomato
1½ oz. canned bamboo shoots
2 oz. Chinese mushrooms (see page 150)
2 oz. canned water chestnuts
1½ pints (U.S. 3¾ cups) beef stock
  (see page 36)
pinch salt, pinch Ve-Tsin (see page 151)

Prepare the onion garnish as directed and drop the pieces into very cold, preferably iced, water until required.
Cut the rump steak into thin strips on the bias — that is, almost across the grain. Cut the tomato into 4 slices. Thinly slice the bamboo shoots, mushrooms (stalks discarded) and water chestnuts.
Bring the stock to the boil. Add the meat and cook for 4-5 minutes. Add the vegetables and boil for 1 minute. Add the seasonings and boil for a further minute. Turn the soup into a tureen. Shake the moisture from the 'flowers' and garnish the soup with them.

Note

When green spring onions are not available, substitute 4 small sprigs of watercress.

YIN WOR TONG
BIRDS' NEST SOUP

Preparation time   overnight plus 6 minutes
Cooking time   1 hour 5 minutes
To serve   3-4

You will need

1 oz. birds' nests (see page 150)
1 oz. finely chopped raw white chicken meat
1 oz. finely chopped lean boiled ham
1¾ pints (U.S. 4¼ cups) very rich chicken stock
salt to taste
1 small teaspoon cornflour
1 tablespoon water
1 beaten egg white

Well cover the birds' nests with cold water and leave them to soak overnight.
Finely chop the chicken meat and ham (which should have no fat in it) and keep them separate.
Drain the birds' nests. Remove and discard any feathers then rinse and drain the nests again. Turn the nests into a pot and add the cold stock. Bring to the boil, then cover and simmer for 1 hour. Taste and, if necessary, add salt.
If the stock has boiled down too much add hot water — not more stock because that would increase the saltiness too much.
Add the chicken meat and cook for 3 minutes. Blend the cornflour with the water, stir it in and boil for 1½ minutes.
Remove from heat and whisk in beaten egg white. Turn the soup into a tureen or individual bowls; sprinkle the ham on top and serve at once.

NGOW YUG TONG
BEEF STOCK

Cut 1 lb. leg beef into small dice or strips. Put them in a pot. Add 2 pints (U.S. 5 cups) water and a little salt and pepper. Cover closely, bring slowly to the boil, then simmer very gently for 2 hours. Strain and use in any soup where beef stock is required. For speed, and when you do not have a beef stock on hand, use a good quality beef bouillon cube and water to produce a clear stock.

NGOW YUK HAM CHOY TONG
BEEF AND MUSTARD PLANT SOUP

Preparation time 4-6 minutes
Cooking time 5-6 minutes
To serve 4

You will need

1½-2 pints (U.S. 3¾-5 cups) beef stock
   or 2 beef stock cubes and water
3-4 tablespoons lean beef
pinch each pepper, salt and Ve-Tsin
   (see page 151)
good pinch sugar
1 teaspoon ginger sherry (see page 151)
½ teaspoon cornflour
1 dessertspoon water
3 tablespoons salted mustard plant (canned)

Cut the meat, on the bias, into very thin slices. Turn them into a basin with the seasonings, sugar and ginger sherry. Mix well together. Blend the cornflour with the water and work it well into the beef. Set aside for the time being.
Cut the mustard plant into thin slices. Bring the beef stock to the boil. Add the beef and mustard plant and boil for 3-4 minutes. Serve at once.

YUK PIN TONG
PORK AND LEEK SOUP

Preparation time 8-10 minutes
Cooking time 8-10 minutes
To serve 4

You will need

4 tablespoons thinly sliced lean raw pork
pinch each salt, sugar and Ve-Tsin
½-1 teaspoon ginger sherry (see page 151)
1½ teaspoons cornflour
1 fair-sized leek
1¾-2 pints (U.S. 4¼-5 cups) chicken stock
   (see below) *
1 tablespoon water

* Use the stock from a boiled chicken or that made from chicken giblets or water and 2 chicken stock cubes, following the directions on the packet.

Have the pork in one piece from the leg or blade bone (English cut).
Place it flat on the table and cut it diagonally into the thinnest possible slices. (This will help to keep them flat in the cooking rather than curled). Place them in a small bowl.
Add the seasonings and sherry and work them together, then add 1 teaspoon cornflour and work it well in. Set aside for the time.
Use only the white part of the leek. Having washed it very well, cut it into very, very thin slices.
Meanwhile, bring the stock to the boil.
Add the leek and boil until the pieces are translucent. Add the pork and cook for 5-6 minutes, because the meat is so very thinly cut.
Blend the remaining cornflour with the water, stir it into the soup and boil for 1½ minutes.
Serve at once.

Sweet corn and chicken soup; chicken and bamboo shoots; egg drop soup

Paper wrapped and deep fat fried prawns

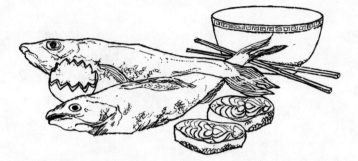

FISH AND SHELLFISH

YU; YIN, HAR, HAI

For me, the charm of Chinese sea-food is the way in which vegetables are combined with it to make more of the fish itself. Each is independent of the other — yet each depends on the other for the excellence of the dish.

While we rarely, if ever, cook fish and vegetables together, the Chinese, for the most part, do just that. There is another very important point: in some Chinese dishes, fresh ginger is cooked for half a minute in the oil in which the fish is to be fried and then discarded. This, in some subtle way, diminishes the fishy flavour and makes the dish more acceptable to those who do not care for sea-foods.

Shellfish, from shrimps to lobsters, is very important in the Chinese kitchen. Lobster is expensive anywhere in the world but the Chinese cook can make one go very much further than any other chef — and, I think, to greater advantage.

JEE BOW HAR

PAPER-WRAPPED AND DEEP FAT FRIED PRAWNS

(Illustrated in colour on page 38)

Preparation time 10-15 minutes
Cooking time 5 minutes
To serve 3

You will need

shredded lettuce heart
2 raw Pacific prawns
1 small clove garlic
1 thin slice fresh ginger root
pinch pepper
½ teaspoon sesame oil
½ teaspoon ginger sherry (see page 151)
salt to taste
pinch Ve-Tsin (see page 151)
½ egg white
good pinch cornflour
1 tablespoon canned bamboo shoots
peanut oil

Cut the lettuce into thin strips and place them on a serving dish.

After removing the black intestinal lines, finely chop the prawns.

Add the finely chopped garlic and ginger and then the pepper, sesame oil, sherry, salt, Ve-Tsin, egg white and cornflour. Mix very well together with the finger tips.

Finally, add the finely chopped bamboo shots. Have ready six 6-inch squares of greaseproof paper, each rubbed with a little peanut oil.

Place one-sixth of the mixture towards one corner of each.

Fold over this corner and then the two sides and tuck in the remaining flap.

Heat enough peanut oil for deep frying. Test by dropping a piece of potato into it. It should rise but not bounce up.

Lower the 'packets' into it and cook for 5 minutes when they will be beautifully brown. Place on the bed of lettuce.

Unwrap each 'packet' and eat from the paper.

DAN CHIN HAR

EGG-COATED
AND FRIED PRAWNS

Preparation time   5 minutes
Cooking time   5 minutes
To serve   2

You will need

3 frozen Pacific prawns
little pepper
pinch salt
pinch sugar
good pinch Ve-Tsin (see page 151)
1 beaten egg
2 tablespoons peanut oil
lettuce

Halve the shelled prawns lengthwise. Remove the black intestinal lines and trim off tails and rough edges. Mix together the pepper, salt, sugar and Ve-Tsin. Dust the prawns with them and work them well in. Add the egg and mix well.
Heat the oil. Fry the prawns in it for 2 minutes on each side.
Arrange the lettuce leaves on a serving dish and place the fried prawns on them.

Note

If it becomes necessary to add a little extra oil — and it often is because the Chinese cook uses as little of it as possible — add it down the inside of the pan and never over the ingredients.

DOW SEE HAR KOW

PACIFIC PRAWNS
AND BLACK SOYA BEANS

Preparation time   5 minutes
Cooking time   4 minutes
To serve   3-4

You will need

5-6 frozen Pacific prawns
tiny pinch black pepper
pinch each sugar and salt
good pinch Ve-Tsin (see page 151)
2 tablespoons peanut oil
3 crushed thin slices fresh ginger
1 crushed clove garlic
2 tablespoons canned black soya beans
$\frac{1}{4}$ pint (U.S. $\frac{2}{3}$ cup) chicken stock
1 teaspoon soy sauce
1 level teaspoon cornflour
1 dessertspoon water
1 onion 'flower' (see opposite)
parsley sprigs

Halve the shelled prawns and remove the black intestinal lines.
Cut the prawns diagonally into $\frac{1}{2}$-to $\frac{3}{4}$-inch pieces. Sprinkle with the pepper, sugar, salt and Ve-Tsin and work them well in.
Heat the peanut oil. Add the ginger and garlic, cook till pale gold colour and then discard. Add the beans and cook for less than $\frac{1}{2}$ minute, tossing and turning them. Add the prawns and cook all for 2 minutes, moving them about. Add the hot stock, soy sauce and cornflour blended with the water.

Pacific prawns and black soya beans

Boil for 1-1½ minutes.
Turn into a suitable heated dish and garnish with the onion 'flower' and parsley.

TO MAKE THE ONION 'FLOWERS'

Cut four 1½- to 2-inch lengths of firm green spring onion stalks; cut down one-third way from each end. Drop them into cold iced water. The ends will spring out into circular 'flowers'.

HAR MAI FAN SEE

FRIED PRAWNS
WITH TRANSPARENT NOODLES

Preparation time 25 minutes
Cooking time   11-12 minutes
To serve   3

You will need

1 oz. dried Chinese prawns (see page 151)
3 Mungo bean sticks (see page 151)
2 oz. transparent noodles
2 oz. raw pork
6 whole watercress leaves or ¼-inch strips lettuce
1 tablespoon peanut oil
¼ pint (U.S. ⅔ cup) chicken stock *
pinch each salt, sugar and Ve-Tsin (see page 151)
1 onion 'flower' (see below)

* If you have no chicken stock available use 1 chicken bouillon cube and water.

Soak the prawns for 20 minutes in cold water.
Soak the Mungo beans sticks for a few minutes in boiling water and the transparent noodles for 2 minutes in cold water.
Drain all three.
Cut the raw pork into very thin strips. Have ready the watercress leaves or equivalent quantity of lettuce strips.
Cook the pork for 2 minutes in the hot peanut oil.
Add the chicken stock, salt, sugar and Ve-Tsin and then the bean sticks and prawns. Cook for 8 minutes.
Lastly, add the noodles and watercress or lettuce and cook for 2 minutes.
Turn into a heated serving dish and garnish with the onion 'flower'.

TO MAKE THE ONION 'FLOWER'

Cut four 1½- to 2-inch lengths of firm green spring onion stalks, then cut down one-third way from each end.
Drop them into cold iced water and the ends will spring out into circular fringes or 'flowers'.

Fried prawns with transparent noodles

Fried prawns and pork fat

Creamed crab with bamboo shoots

WOR DIP HAR
FRIED PRAWNS AND PORK FAT

Preparation time   20 minutes
Cooking time   15 minutes
To serve   3-4

You will need

6 frozen Pacific prawns
6 paper thin slices back pork fat
pinch each pepper, salt and sugar
good pinch Ve-Tsin (see page 151)
2 beaten egg yolks
3 tablespoons cornflour
peanut oil
heart of lettuce leaves

Cut the shelled prawns almost through lengthwise. Remove the black intestinal lines and trim off rough edges. Flatten out each prawn. Divide it into 6 rectangular pieces, each just short of the full length of a prawn and a trifle narrower than the widest part. Mix together the seasonings and work them into the prawns. Lay them opened sides up. Draw each piece of pork fat on one side only through the beaten eggs and place it, egged side down, on a prawn. (The egg will hold the two together.) Dip each portion in the cornflour, shake off excess, then dip in the egg yolks and again in the cornflour.

In a frying-pan heat peanut oil to a depth of $\frac{1}{2}$ inch. When fairly hot, place the prawns in it, pork side down, and fry until golden. Turn and fry the other sides to a golden tone at a little less heat. Arrange portions on lettuce heart and serve.

HAI YUK SAN SEE
CREAMED CRAB WITH BAMBOO SHOOTS

Preparation time   5 minutes
Cooking time   6 minutes
To serve   2

You will need

2 tablespoons peanut oil
3 oz. canned bamboo shoots, cut into strips
salt, sugar and Ve-Tsin (see page 151)
2-3 oz. flaked cooked white crab meat
$\frac{1}{2}$ teaspoon ginger sherry (see page 151)
$\frac{1}{4}$ pint (U.S. $\frac{2}{3}$ cup) chicken stock
1 teaspoon cornflour
1 dessertspoon water
2 tablespoons milk
1 sprig parsley or watercress

Heat half the oil in a frying-pan. Add bamboo shoots, season with a pinch of salt, sugar and Ve-Tsin and cook for 3 minutes, stirring. Turn into a heated dish. Wipe out the pan. Add the remaining oil. When hot, add the crab meat and, as it cooks add the sherry, stock and another pinch salt, sugar and Ve-Tsin, tossing and turning all for $\frac{1}{4}$ minute. Add the cornflour, blended with the water, and stir while it comes to the boil. Add the milk and bring to the boil again.

Lastly, return the bamboo shoots to the pan and heat through for $\frac{1}{4}$ minute. Turn all into a heated serving dish and garnish with a sprig of parsley or watercress.

Prawns with mixed vegetables

SIN HAR SUB GUM
PRAWNS
WITH MIXED VEGETABLES

Preparation time   10 minutes
Cooking time   8-10 minutes
To serve   4

You will need

4 sliced shelled raw Pacific prawns
3 teaspoons cornflour
pinch each pepper and sugar
salt
good pinch Ve-Tsin (see page 151)
1 dessertspoon sesame oil
3 oz. carrot
3 oz. cucumber
3 oz. bamboo shoots
2-3 water chestnuts
2 tablespoons peanut oil
¼ pint (U.S. ⅔ cup) chicken stock
    (preferably hot)
1 dessertspoon water

Put the sliced prawns (black intestinal lines removed) in a basin and sprinkle them with 2 teaspoons cornflour, a pinch of salt and other seasonings and sesame oil. Mix well together.
Cut the vegetables into thin strips and season them with salt only. Fry them, moving them about, for 3 minutes in 1 tablespoon of the peanut oil. Add the stock and cook for another 3 minutes. Transfer all to a heated dish.
Wipe clean the pan and in it heat the remaining oil.
Cook the prawns in the oil for 1½-2 minutes,

moving them about.
Drain the liquid from the vegetables into the pan and bring to the boil. Add 1 teaspoon cornflour, blended with the water. Bring to the boil again and simmer for 1-1½ minutes.
Add the vegetables and turn all into a deep heated serving dish.

FAR SAN MAN SIEN
EEL WITH PEANUTS

Preparation time   10 minutes
Cooking time   7-8 minutes
To serve   3-4

You will need

salt
1 12 oz.-1 lb. eel
pinch Ve-Tsin (see page 151)
1 teaspoon ginger sherry (see page 151)
1 rounded teaspoon cornflour
peanut oil
2 finely chopped thin slices fresh ginger
1 crushed clove garlic
4 tablespoons hot chicken stock
3 oz. skinned roasted peanuts

Rub 2-3 teaspoons salt well into the eel and leave to rest for 1-2 minutes. This will get rid of the viscous coating.
Wash well. Cut down the belly and clean the eel. Wash again and dry.
Cut the eel into 1-inch slices across the bone. Work into them a pinch of salt and a pinch of Ve-Tsin and the ginger sherry then rub them through the cornflour.
Have enough oil to deep fry heated to 385°F. or 196°C. or to the stage when a slice of raw potato or onion dropped into it rests for a few seconds then rises to the surface.
Fry the pieces of eel in it for 3 minutes. Lift out and drain well.
Heat 1 tablespoon oil in a frying-pan. Add the ginger and garlic. Cook until the garlic is golden and then discard it.
Add the pieces of eel, hot stock and peanuts. Cover and cook for 4 minutes at a high heat. If necessary, add a little more stock, but only a little sauce is needed for this dish.

Pacific prawns and tomato sauce

KAY JOP HAR KOW
PACIFIC PRAWNS
AND TOMATO SAUCE

Preparation time   5 minutes
Cooking time   4 minutes
To serve   4

You will need

5-6 frozen Pacific prawns
2 tablespoons peanut oil
1 crushed slice fresh ginger
1 crushed clove garlic
pinch each salt, pepper, sugar and Ve-Tsin
  see page 151)
$\frac{1}{2}$ teaspoon ginger sherry (see page 151)
1 rounded tablespoon tomato ketchup
$\frac{1}{4}$ pint (U.S. $\frac{2}{3}$ cup) chicken stock
$\frac{3}{4}$ teaspoon cornflour
1 dessertspoon water
1 onion 'flower' (see page 46)
sprigs parsley

Cut through the shelled prawns and remove the black intestinal lines. Slice the prawns into 1-inch pieces.
Heat the oil. While it is getting hot, add the ginger and garlic and let them begin to colour. Then remove them.
Add the prawns and move them about as they cook for 1 minute.
Add the seasonings, ginger sherry, tomato ketchup and chicken stock and cook for 1 minute. Add the cornflour, blended with the water, and cook for

a further 2 minutes. Taste and, if necessary, add further salt and Ve-Tsin.
Turn the mixture into a heated serving dish and garnish with the onion 'flower' and sprigs of parsley.

TONG CHO HAR
SWEET AND SOUR PRAWNS

Preparation time   5 minutes
Cooking time   4 minutes
To serve   2-3

You will need

3-4 oz. frozen Dublin Bay prawns (scampi)
1 dessertspoon flour
1 small onion
2 tablespoons pineapple wedges
2 tablespoons ripe tomato, cut in wedges
1 tablespoon green sweet pepper, diced
$\frac{1}{4}$ small hot red chilli
1 tablespoon peanut oil
1 teaspoon tomato purée
2 small tablespoons sugar
salt
2 tablespoons wine vinegar
1 small teaspoon cornflour
1 dessertspoon water

Defrost the prawns and work in the flour. Set them aside.
Chop the onion, pineapple and tomato and green pepper and pound the chilli to a paste.
Heat the peanut oil and quickly fry the scampi in it to a golden tone.
Lift out and fry the onion, tossing it about to cook but not colour.
Add the tomato purée, sugar, chilli paste, and season lightly with salt.
Add the chicken stock, vinegar and cornflour blended with the water.
Cook for 1$\frac{1}{2}$ minutes.
Add the tomatoes, green pepper and pineapple wedges. Heat through. Add the scampi with a tiny pinch of salt. Move about gently.
Heat through and serve.

44

CHENE DOW HAR YEN
PRAWNS WITH PEAS

Preparation time   4-5 minutes
Cooking time   4-5 minutes
To serve   3-4

You will need

1 slice fresh ginger
1 clove garlic
2 tablespoons peanut oil
4 oz. shelled cooked prawns
¼ pint (U.S. ⅔ cup) chicken stock*
pinch each salt, sugar and Ve-Tsin
   (see page 151)
1 teaspoon soy sauce
5-6 oz. cooked peas
1 level teaspoon cornflour
1 dessertspoon water

* If chicken stock is not available use 1 chicken
bouillon cube with water.

Crush the fresh ginger and crush the clove of
garlic.
Place the peanut oil in a large frying-pan. Before
it becomes really hot, add the crushed ginger and
crushed garlic. Cook until the garlic takes on a pale
gold tone then remove it together with the ginger.
Add the cooked prawns, cook for ½ minute then
add the chicken stock, the salt, sugar, Ve-Tsin, soy
sauce and, finally, the peas and the cornflour

blended with the water. Cook for 1½ minutes. Turn
the mixture into a deep heated dish and serve.

HAR BENG
PRAWN CRACKERS

Prawn crackers are sometimes known as shrimp
slices and are obtainable from any store specialising
in oriental foods as well as from other high-class
establishments where such goods are not normally
sold. They appear to be oval discs, not larger than
a man's thumb nail.
Prawn crackers are dropped, a few at a time, into
hot peanut or other vegetable oil. They should
rise fairly quickly and expand into large deep petal
shapes, several times larger than their original size.
They should not colour. The first few crackers may
not be successful but very soon one becomes quite
expert in deep-fat frying them at the right temperature and for the correct length of time. I do not
use a thermometer but test the heat of the oil in the
following way:
I drop a very thin slice of dried raw potato into
the peanut or vegetable oil. If it rests for a few
seconds at the bottom of the pan and then rises
to the surface, the temperature is right. If, however,
the crackers are slightly tinted and smaller than
you remember seeing them at Fu Tong's or other
good Chinese restaurants, you may be sure that the
oil was too hot.

Prawns with peas

DIM SIN LOO YU

SWEET-SOUR SEA BASS

(Illustrated in colour on opposite page)
Preparation time   10 minutes
Cooking time   10-15 minutes
To serve   4-5

You will need

1 1-1¼ lb. sea bass
pinch salt
pinch Ve-Tsin (see page 151)
tiny pinch pepper
1 teaspoon sesame oil
1 teaspoon ginger sherry (see page 151)
2-3 tablespoons self-raising flour
peanut oil for deep frying
sweet-sour sauce (see below)
8-10 onion 'flowers' (see below)

Scale and clean the fish through the gills. Dry it, inside and out, and sprinkle it, inside and out, with the salt, Ve-Tsin and pepper, mixed together. Dab the fish here and there with the sesame oil and ginger sherry.

Have the oil deep enough for the fish to be submerged in it. Heat it to the stage where a slice of raw potato does not at once rise to the surface when it is dropped into the oil. The temperature will then be 350-360°F. or 176°-182°C. which is correct for raw fish. It will require 10-15 minutes. Raise the temperature towards the end of cooking so that the fish will be golden in colour.

Place the well drained bass on a heated oval dish, arrange the sweet-sour sauce around it and garnish with the onion 'flowers'.

SWEET-SOUR SAUCE

1 tablespoon sugar
pinch salt
pinch pepper
pinch Ve-Tsin (see page 151)
3 tablespoons malt vinegar
1 teaspoon soy sauce
1 teaspoon tomato ketchup
scant ¼ pint (U.S. ½ cup) water
1 teaspoon cornflour
1 dessertspoon water
2 tablespoons Chinese pickles

Bring the first eight ingredients to the boil. Stir in the cornflour, blended with the dessertspoon water

and boil for 2 minutes, stirring continuously. Add the pickles and heat through.

TO MAKE THE ONION 'FLOWERS'

Cut four 1½- to 2-inch lengths of firm green spring onion stalks, then cut down one-third way from each end.
Drop them into cold iced water and the ends will spring into circular fringes or 'flowers'.

YUNG WOO TOW

STUFFED GREY MULLET

Preparation time   20 minutes
Cooking time   15 minutes
To serve   3-4

You will need

1 12 oz. - 1 lb. grey mullet
1 small thin slice fresh ginger
1 spring onion
good pinch each salt and Ve-Tsin
  (see page 151)
several shakes pepper
1 teaspoon ginger sherry*
2 Pacific prawns, cleaned and chopped
1 teaspoon cornflour

* Cut 2 oz. fresh ginger into thin strips. Turn them into a bottle and cover with ½ bottle warm brown sherry. Leave to infuse, strain and use as directed.

Scale and wash the mullet. Cut through the belly and remove the insides.
Break the spinebone at the head and tail ends and carefully remove it. Remove the flesh away from the skin on both sides, leaving the head and tail intact.
Pick out and discard any small bones remaining in the flesh. Chop the flesh.
Add the finely chopped ginger and onion, seasonings and sherry and the prawns. Mix all together to a smooth paste.
Spread the mullet, inside up, on a board and sprinkle the cornflour all over it. Add the paste and bring the skin on each side over it to shape the fish into its original form, patting it well so that the skin will adhere to the stuffing.
Place the fish on an oiled oval plate, steam it for 15 minutes and serve.

Sweet-sour sea bass

Fried fillets of Dover sole and garnish

SUB GUM YU PIN

FRIED FILLETS OF DOVER SOLE AND GARNISH

(Illustrated in colour on opposite page)

Preparation time 6-7 minutes
Cooking time 10-12 minutes
To serve 4

You will need

1 skinned and filleted 1½-lb. sole
½-¾ teaspoon ginger sherry (see page 151)
1 teaspoon sesame oil
⅓ teaspoon salt
¼ teaspoon sugar
¼ teaspoon Ve-Tsin (see page 151)
1 teaspoon cornflour
1 tablespoon water
½ egg white

THE GARNISH

1 small onion
1 medium-sized green sweet pepper
1 medium-sized red sweet pepper
2 firm ripe small tomatoes
2 tablespoons peanut oil
1 clove garlic
2 thin slices fresh ginger
1 teaspoon soy sauce
pinch each salt, pepper, Ve-Tsin and sugar
1-2 onion 'flowers' (see below)

Cut the sole diagonally into 1- to 1½-inch slices. Add and work in the next 8 ingredients. (Watching a Chinese cook do this is fascinating. He picks up the pieces of sole with his finger tips, drops them back again and leaves them while preparing the garnish.)
Cut the onion into thickish pieces and separate them. Cut the washed peppers into wide slices, discarding seeds and stringy bits. Quarter the tomatoes. Heat the oil in a pan large enough for all the ingredients. Add the crushed garlic and ginger, leave for ½ minute then flick them out. Add and cook the onion pieces for ½ minute, moving them about. Add the pepper pieces and gently move all about for 1 minute over fairly high heat. Lastly, add the tomatoes and seasonings, move gently about for ½ minute and set aside. Lower the pieces of sole into deep oil before it is too hot, because they must be cooked through with only slight colouring; 4-5 minutes should be ample. Drain well. Add to the vegetables and cook together for ½ minute.

Turn all on to a heated serving dish and garnish with the onion 'flowers'.

TO MAKE THE ONION 'FLOWERS'

Cut four 1½- to 2-inch lengths of firm green spring onion stalks, then cut down one-third way from each end. Drop them into cold iced water and the ends will spring out into circular fringes or 'flowers'.

GON SIEW HAR

PRAWNS SHANGHAIENNES

Preparation time 5 minutes
Cooking time 6 minutes
To serve 3-4

You will need

6 Pacific prawns
1-2 beaten eggs
salt
1 medium-sized finely chopped onion
¼ small hot red chilli
peanut oil
1 small dessertspoon sugar
pinch Ve-Tsin (see page 151)
1 teaspoon tomato purée
2 tablespoons chicken stock
1 small teaspoon cornflour
1 dessertspoon water

Shell, clean and cut the prawns into three pieces each and dip in enough beaten egg with a pinch of salt to seal it. Leave aside. Finely chop the onion. Pound the chilli with 1-2 drops oil. Heat 2 table-spoons oil in a frying-pan. Add the prawns; toss and move them about for 2 minutes. Lift them out and drain and in the pan, with hardly any oil in it, fry the onion, tossing and moving it about, until it is translucent but not coloured. Away from the heat add the chilli, the sugar, Ve-Tsin, tomato purée and pinch salt and mix well together. Add stock then the prawns and cook for 2 minutes. Finally blend the cornflour and the water. Cook for 1½ minutes.

Tong Yen uses Dublin Bay prawns (scampi) for Prawns Shanghaiennes. In England where Pacific prawns are available and less expensive we use them. Crawfish or lobster are just as suitable but much more expensive.

49

Lobster with rice noodles

LOONG HAR CHOW MAI
LOBSTER WITH RICE NOODLES

Preparation time 10 minutes
Cooking time 10 minutes
To serve 2-3

You will need

1 1¼-lb. lobster or 2 small frozen crawfish tails
1 oz. rice noodles
1 small onion
2 tablespoons raw celery
1 Chinese mushroom, soaked overnight
  (see page 150)
2 tablespoons canned bamboo shoots
1 small green sweet pepper
3 tablespoons peanut oil
pinch each salt, sugar and Ve-Tsin
  (see page 151)
1 teaspoon ginger sherry (see page 151)
1 teaspoon soy sauce
¼ pint (U.S. ⅝ cup) chicken stock
1 teaspoon cornflour
1 dessertspoon water

Remove the crawfish tails from the shells. After discarding the black intestinal lines cut the tails into strips. Cook the noodles for 5 minutes in boiling water. Chop the onion and slice the other vegetables. Heat 2 tablespoons oil and fry the crawfish pieces in it for 1 minute. Drain the noodles and add to the crawfish with further oil, if necessary, and fry them until golden, shaping them to the serving dish. Turn the crawfish and noodles into the heated dish and keep hot.
Add the rest of the oil to the pan and make it hot.

Fry the onion in it for ½ minute then add the celery, mushroom and bamboo shoots in that order, allowing ¼ minute for each addition. Then add the green pepper and cook for a further minute. Add the seasonings, sherry and soy sauce and toss and turn to blend them with the vegetables. Add the stock and cook for ½ minute. Add the cornflour, blended with the water, and boil for 1½ minutes. Pour all this over the crawfish and noodles and serve.

LOONG HAR KOW
LOBSTER BALLS

Preparation time 6-7 minutes
Cooking time 7-9 minutes
To serve 3

You will need

3 oz. self-raising flour
1 small egg
¼ pint (U.S. ⅝ cup) water
12 oz. raw lobster*
pinch each pepper, salt, sugar and Ve-Tsin
  (see page 151)
1 tablespoon cornflour
peanut oil for deep frying
parsley to garnish

* Lobster is given here but crawfish or Pacific prawns can be used instead.

First, make the batter. Sift the flour into a basin, work in the egg and gradually beat in the water. Leave to rest for an hour or so.
Prepare the shellfish. Cut it into suitable pieces, trim off any ragged bits and discard the black intestinal lines. Dust with the seasonings and roll in the cornflour. Coat with the batter and drain off excess.
Gradually heat the oil which should be deep enough to cover the 'balls' when they are dropped into it. The oil should be hot enough to colour the surface and also cook the raw lobster through — about 7-8 minutes.
Drain, transfer to a heated serving dish and garnish with parsley.

VARIATION
Heat ¼ pint (U.S. ⅝ cup) of sweet-sour sauce (see page 46). Gently roll the drained 'balls' on absorbent paper then drop them into the sauce and heat through.

50

Lobster balls

HONG SHU LOO YEE
FRIED BASS WITH VEGETABLE GARNISH

Preparation time   12-15 minutes
Cooking time   10-12 minutes (fish),
                     5 minutes (vegetables)
To serve   4

You will need

1 1¼-1½ lb. sea bass, scaled and cleaned
salt and pepper
1 beaten egg
2 tablespoons plain flour
peanut oil
1½ tablespoons lean pork
1 onion
1 tablespoon carrot
1 tablespoon bamboo shoots
1 Chinese mushroom (see page 150)
1 tablespoon Szechwan cabbage (see page 79)
pinch sugar
¼ teaspoon Ve-Tsin (see page 151)
1-1½ teaspoons soy sauce
¼ pint (U.S. ⅝ cup) chicken stock
scant ¾ teaspoon cornflour
1 tablespoon water.

Scrape from fish off any dark inside skin, sprinkle
the inside and outside with salt and pepper. Have
ready the egg and flour on separate plates.
Cut the pork into fairly thin slices and the vegetables into thin strips.
Place enough peanut oil for deep frying in a deep
pan wide enough to contain the fish and get it

fairly hot. Dip the fish in the egg and then the
flour. Lower it into the oil and cook it for 10-12
minutes.
After the fish has been cooking for a few minutes,
start to cook the garnish. Heat 2 tablespoons of
peanut oil in a large frying-pan. Cook the onion in
the oil for ½ minute. Add the pork and cook for
1½ minutes, then add the remaining vegetables
and keep moving them about. If the vegetables
seem to be cooking too much, lower the heat. Add
a pinch of salt, sugar and the Ve-Tsin, stock and
cornflour blended with the water. Cook for about
3 minutes. Place the drained fish on a heated dish
and pour the garnish over it.

Fried bass with vegetable garnish

Sweet and sour trout

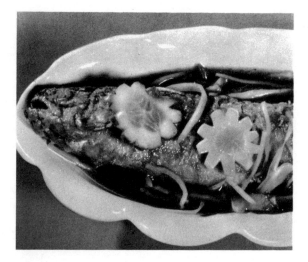

DIM SIN CHO YEE
SWEET AND SOUR TROUT

Preparation time   5 minutes
Cooking time   12-15 minutes
To serve   3

You will need

1 8-9 oz. trout
sprinkle pepper
pinch salt
good pinch Ve-Tsin (see page 151)
1 beaten egg
2 tablespoons self-raising flour
2 tablespoons thinly sliced boiled carrots
3 slices raw cucumber
fairly hot deep peanut oil

SWEET-SOUR SAUCE

1 tablespoon sugar
pinch each salt and pepper
good pinch Ve-Tsin
3 tablespoons malt vinegar
1 teaspoon soy sauce
1 teaspoon tomato ketchup
scant $\frac{1}{4}$ pint (U.S. $\frac{5}{8}$ cup) water
1 teaspoon cornflour
1 dessertspoon water

Ask the fishmonger to scrape the trout and remove the insides through the gills, leaving the head on. Sprinkle inside and out with the pepper, salt and Ve-Tsin. Beat the egg. Have the flour ready on a plate. Cut the sliced carrots into thin strips. Slice the unpeeled cucumber and cut nicks all round the slices.

Coat the trout all over with the egg and then pass it through the flour. Lower the fish into the hot oil (350-360°F. or 176°-182°C.) remembering that it is raw and must be cooked all through without being browned too quickly. Give it 12-15 minutes. While the fish is cooking, make the sauce. Mix together the first 7 ingredients. Bring to the boil. Stir in the cornflour, blended with the water and boil for 2 minutes while stirring. Add the prepared vegetables and heat through. Place the drained trout on a heated deep dish. Pour the sauce and vegetables over it and serve.

KAY JOP MUN YEE
BRAISED TURBOT
WITH TOMATO

Preparation time   8 minutes
Cooking time   15 minutes
To serve   2

You will need

2 thin slices turbot, from tail end
1 tomato*
good pinch salt
good pinch Ve-Tsin (see page 151)
pinch sugar
2-3 tablespoons peanut oil
4 tablespoons chicken stock
$\frac{1}{2}$ teaspoon cornflour
1 dessertspoon water
1 teaspoon tomato ketchup
1 sprig parsley

* Make sure the tomato is firm-skinned and ripe.

Trim off any fin bones from the fish. Vandyke the tomato. Hold it in one hand. With a very sharp slender pointed knife in the other, cut 'V's and inverted 'V's all round from half-way down the tomato right through to the centre. The two halves will then come away clean and attractively serrated.

Mix the salt, Ve-Tsin and sugar. Sprinkle the fish on both sides with the seasonings. For 6 minutes fry the slices on both sides in the oil. Add the chicken stock and cook gently for 5 minutes. Add the tomato halves and cook for 2 minutes. Add the cornflour, blended with the water, and turn the pan this way and that to incorporate it. Lift the fish on to a heated dish and place a halved tomato at each end. Add the tomato ketchup to the sauce and boil up. Spoon this over the fish and tomato and garnish with the sprig of parsley.

Braised turbot with tomato

Steamed halibut with vegetables

VING LEE

STEAMED HALIBUT WITH VEGETABLES

Preparation time 5 minutes
Cooking time 10-15 minutes
To serve 4

You will need

2 small slices halibut
3 thin slices fresh ginger
1 soaked Chinese mushroom (see page 150)
1 spring onion
2 tablespoons shredded Szechwan cabbage
 (see page 79)
1 dessertspoon shredded cooked lean pork
little pepper
pinch each sugar and salt
good pinch Ve-Tsin (see page 151)
1 teaspoon sesame oil
1 dessertspoon soy sauce
1 teaspoon cornflour
1 dessertspoon water
1 onion 'flower' (see page 49)

Place the trimmed halibut ready on a plate. Cut the ginger and mushroom (stem discarded) into thin strips. Cut on the slant the spring onion into ¾-inch pieces. Add the cabbage, pork and seasonings, then the oil, soy sauce and cornflour, blended with the water. Mix well together. Heap on to the halibut slices and steam for 10-15 minutes. Transfer carefully to a heated serving dish. Remove skin and

bones. If necessary, rearrange the vegetables. Garnish with the onion 'flower'.

GIN WONG JOP

FRIED HERRINGS

Preparation time 3-4 minutes
Cooking time 6-7 minutes
To serve 3

You will need

3 small herrings
good pinch salt
good pinch Ve-Tsin (see page 151)
few shakes pepper
1 dessertspoon self-raising flour
2 tablespoons peanut oil
1 spring onion
few dashes soy sauce

Scrape, de-gut and wash the herrings, leaving the heads and tails on. Add the salt, Ve-Tsin and pepper to the flour and pass the herrings through the mixture.
Heat the oil in a frying-pan. Fry the herrings in it on both sides.
While they are cooking, finely chop the onion. Drain the fish on absorbent paper.
Place on a heated serving dish and sprinkle with the onion and soy sauce.

LOONG HAR SUB GUM

CRAWFISH AND MIXED VEGETABLES

Preparation time 10 minutes
Cooking time 6-7 minutes
To serve 3-4

You will need

4 tablespoons sliced shelled frozen crawfish*
3 teaspoons cornflour
sprinkle pepper
salt, sugar
good pinch Ve-Tsin (see page 151)
1 teaspoon soy sauce
1 teaspoon sesame oil
1 teaspoon ginger sherry (see below 151)
3 tablespoons cucumber
3 tablespoons carrots
3 tablespoons canned bamboo shoots
3 tablespoons canned water chestnuts
2-3 tablespoons peanut oil
¼ pint (U.S. ⅝ cup) chicken stock**
1 dessertspoon water

* Other shellfish, such as lobster, Pacific prawns and even scallops when seasonable, can be used in the same way.

** If there is no chicken stock available use 1 chicken bouillon cube and water.

First prepare the crawfish. Mix very well with 2 teaspoons cornflour, pinch salt and sugar, Ve-Tsin, soy sauce, sesame oil and ginger sherry. Leave for the time being.

Cut the sliced vegetables into strips and keep the raw ones and canned ones separate. Heat the oil. Fry the cucumber and carrots in it for 1 minute. Add the bamboo shoots and chestnuts with another pinch of salt and cook for 3 minutes, moving them about. Add the stock. Bring to the boil and stir in the remaining cornflour, blended with the water. Cook for a further 1½ minutes. Turn all into a heated dish and keep hot.

Wipe out the pan. Add 1 tablespoon of peanut oil and make it hot. Turn the crawfish into it and toss and stir for 3 minutes. Add the liquid drained from the vegetables and cook for ½ minute. Add the vegetables and cook for ½ minute. Turn all into a heated dish.

Note

If the sauce tends to be thin, add ½ teaspoon cornflour, blended with 1 teaspoon water, and boil for 1½ minutes before adding the vegetables and proceeding as above.

TO MAKE THE GINGER SHERRY

Cut 1-2 oz. fresh ginger into thin strips. Turn the strips into a bottle and cover with a warm brown sherry. Leave to infuse, strain and use as directed. For 2 oz. fresh ginger, half a bottle of sherry will be the right amount to add.

Crawfish and mixed vegetables

SUNG CHOW-LOONG-HAR

CRAWFISH CANTONESE

Preparation time   5 minutes
Cooking time   8-10 minutes
To serve   2-3

You will need

1 crawfish tail
2 oz. chopped raw pork (lean)
2-3 tablespoons peanut oil
1 crushed clove garlic
½ teaspoon ginger sherry (see page 151)
¼ pint (U.S. ⅝ cup) chicken stock
good pinch each salt, sugar and Ve-Tsin
  (see page 151)
1 dessertspoon - 1 tablespoon tomato ketchup
1 rounded teaspoon cornflour
1 tablespoon water

Remove the under shell of the crawfish tail, leaving the hard shell intact, then cut straight through to include it. Remove the black intestine and then cut the crawfish through in 1-inch slices. Chop the pork. Heat the oil and in it fry the crushed clove of garlic till pale gold and discard it. Fry the pork for 1 minutes add the crawfish pieces and fry them also for 2-3 minutes. Add the ginger sherry, chicken stock, the three seasonings and the tomato ketchup and cook fairly fast for 2-3 minutes. Blend the cornflour and the water, stir it into the pan, bring to the boil and cook for 1½ minutes. Arrange on the serving dish with the shell upwards.

TUNG GOO BOW YEE

AWABI
AND CHINESE MUSHROOMS

Preparation time   3-4 minutes
Cooking time   5 minutes
To serve   2-3

You will need

3 oz. canned awabi
3 oz. Chinese mushrooms (see page 150)
1 tablespoon peanut oil
1 roughly cut up medium-sized onion
1 teaspoon ginger sherry (see page 151)
1 teaspoon sesame oil
¼ pint (U.S. ⅝ cup) chicken stock
pinch sugar
pinch Ve-Tsin (see page 151)
small pinch salt
1 teaspoon soy sauce
½ teaspoon cornflour
1 dessertspoon water

Cut the awabi into thin slices.
Drain and dry the mushrooms (stems removed), leaving them whole.
Heat the oil and fry the onion in it for 1-1½ minutes. Add the awabi and mushrooms and then the next 7 ingredients.
Cook for 2 minutes. Stir the cornflour, blended with the water, into the mixture and boil for 1½-2 minutes.
Turn into a heated dish and serve.

HAR YEN WUI MIN
PRAWNS WITH 'LONG LIFE' NOODLES

Preparation time   10 minutes
Cooking time   10 minutes
To serve   2

You will need

4 Pacific prawns
pinch each salt, sugar and Ve-Tsin
  (see page 151)
1½ teaspoons cornflour
water
4 inside leaves of cos lettuce
2 oz. parboiled 'long life' noodles
2 tablespoons peanut oil
1 clove garlic
1 slice fresh ginger
¼ pint (U.S. ⅝ cup) chicken stock
½ teaspoon soy sauce

Shell and trim the prawns. After removing the black intestinal lines, cut the prawns diagonally into pieces ¾ inch long. Sprinkle them with the seasonings, ½ teaspoon cornflour and 1 teaspoon water and work well into the prawns; leave while proceeding with the rest of the dish. Cut the lettuce into thin strips, pour boiling water over them, leave for 5 minutes and then drain. Boil the noodles for 4-5 minutes and drain them.
Put the oil in a frying-pan. Add the crushed ginger and garlic and heat. When the garlic becomes a golden colour discard it and the ginger. Fry the prawn pieces for 3 minutes, tossing and moving them about. Add the noodles and move them about for 1 minute, then add the stock. Cook together for 4 minutes. Add the lettuce and soy sauce and boil up. Lastly, add 1 teaspoon cornflour, blended with 1 dessertspoon water, and cook all for 1½ minutes.

HAR LUK
FRIED PACIFIC PRAWNS

(Illustrated in colour on opposite page)
Preparation time   6-8 minutes
Cooking time   6-7 minutes
To serve   4

You will need

1 tablespoon ginger sherry*
1 tablespoon sesame oil
1 dessertspoon red bean curd
1 finely chopped fair-sized clove garlic
2 chopped slices fresh ginger
pinch pepper
good pinch salt
good pinch Ve-Tsin (see page 151)
tiny pinch sugar
1 tablespoon beaten egg
8 Pacific prawns
2 tablespoons self-raising flour
2-3 tablespoons peanut oil

* Cut 2 oz. fresh ginger into thin strips. Turn them into a bottle and cover with half bottle warm brown sherry. Leave to infuse, strain and use as directed.

Very well mix together the first 10 ingredients. Put the prawns into the mixture.
Lift the prawns out and sprinkle them with the flour.
In a large frying-pan heat the peanut oil till very hot.
Add the prawns, one at a time.
Shake and turn them into the oil. Lower the heat a little. When the shells are a bright red, the prawns are sufficiently cooked.
Cut through the back of each prawn and remove the black intestinal lines. Transfer to a heated dish and serve.

Fried Pacific prawns

Boned duck, Cantonese style; Phoenix rolls

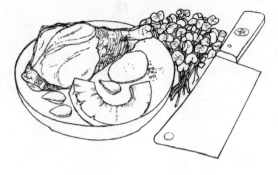

POULTRY

GAI GNAP

Chicken and duck are the principal poultry in the Chinese kitchen and there are innumerable ways in which they can be served, many of them new to the Western world. They range from the simple to the exotic. Some of them would be ideal for appetizers. The most surprising recipe in this section is white cut chicken (see page 61).

Here, the bird is first poached and then cut up and used for several different presentations, two of which are stuffed chicken wings (see page 66) and sweet-sour chicken (see page 69).

The boned duck, Cantonese style, is the only poultry recipe where the whole bird is taken to table. It has been stuffed with the most wonderful cooked savoury mixture, fried just long enough to colour the skin, then steamed until serving portions can be removed with a spoon.

A similar stuffing makes an excellent meat and vegetable dish on its own. It will require a little longer cooking than that given in the recipe to make up for the loss of the cooking time in the duck.

GAI SEE CHOW KAN CHOY
CHICKEN
AND SHREDDED CELERY

Preparation time 6-8 minutes
Cooking time 9-10 minutes
To serve 2-3

You will need

2-3 tablespoons celery
1-2 tablespoons bamboo shoots
2 tablespoons Chinese mushrooms
  (see page 150)
3 tablespoons raw breast of chicken
3 dessertspoons peanut oil
ginger sherry (see page 151)
sesame oil
pepper, salt, sugar and Ve-Tsin
  (see page 151)
2-3 tablespoons stock
½ teaspoon cornflour
1 dessertspoon water

Cut the celery, bamboo shoots, mushrooms and chicken into match-stick pieces and keep them separate. They can be on the one platter as long as they are apart from each other. Heat 2 dessertspoons oil in a frying-pan. Add the celery and toss it about while it cooks for 2 minutes. Add the bamboo shoots and mushrooms and cook them 3 minutes. Add ½ teaspoon sherry, sesame oil and a pinch pepper, salt, sugar and Ve-Tsin and move them about in the pan.

Add the stock and bring it to the boil. Blend the cornflour in the water and stir it in. Boil for 1½ minutes. Turn all into a heated dish.

Wipe out the pan or use another. Add 1 dessertspoon oil and heat it. Toss the chicken in it while it cooks for 1½-2 minutes. Add ¼ teaspoon sherry, few drops sesame oil and a small pinch of pepper, salt, sugar and Ve-Tsin.

Return the vegetable mixture to the pan and move it about as you heat it through. Turn this delicious savoury mixture into a heated dish and serve at once.

TUNG GOO MAN GAI

CHICKEN WITH CHINESE MUSHROOMS

Preparation time   5-6 minutes
Cooking time   4-6 minutes
To serve   2-3

You will need

2-3 tablespoons raw chicken (breast or dark
   meat)
ginger sherry (see page 151)
sesame oil
salt and Ve-Tsin (see page 151)
1 teaspoon cornflour
3 teaspoons water
2 tablespoons thinly sliced Chinese mushrooms
   (see page 150)
2-3 short spears green sprouting broccoli
   peanut oil
1 crushed clove garlic
1 small onion, chopped
3-4 tablespoons hot chicken stock
pinch sugar
¼ teaspoon soy sauce

Cut the raw chicken diagonally into thin slices.
Place them in a bowl with few drops ginger sherry,
few drops sesame oil, tiny pinch salt, tiny pinch
Ve-Tsin, ½ teaspoon cornflour and 1 teaspoon water
and work them very well into the meat with the
finger tips. Leave ready. Also have ready and
separately the stemless mushrooms (cut into thin

strips) and the broccoli spears, which should be
slim and tender rather than thick and coarse.
Heat 1 tablespoon peanut oil in a frying-pan. Add
the garlic and onion. When the onion is a pale gold,
discard the garlic. Add the mushrooms and broccoli
to the pan and move them about for 1½ to 2 minutes.
Meanwhile heat enough oil for deep frying to
375°F. or 190°C. (the ideal temperature for raw
chicken). Drop the chicken slices into it. Add to the
vegetables a few drops ginger sherry, few drops
sesame oil and the chicken stock and cook together
for 3-4 minutes. Add another pinch salt, Ve-Tsin
and the sugar, soy sauce and remaining cornflour,
blended with the rest of the water, and cook for
1½ minutes.
By this time, the chicken pieces should be a rich
golden brown. Lift them out, drain them well and
add them to the vegetables. Turn the mixture into
a heated dish and serve at once.

Note
There is little sauce in this dish but, on the other
hand, it should not be dry. If the mixture does not
seem to be moist enough before adding the cornflour, add 1-2 further tablespoons of stock and
then proceed as above.

BAT SUN GAI DIN

CHICKEN WITH ASPARAGUS

Preparation time   5 minutes
Cooking time   8-9 minutes
To serve   2

You will need

6 tender pieces asparagus
chicken stock*
3 tablespoons raw breast of chicken
1 tablespoon peanut oil
½ teaspoon ginger sherry (see page 151)
¼ pint (U.S. ⅝ cup) chicken stock
½ teaspoon soy sauce
pinch each salt, sugar and Ve-Tsin
   (see page 151)
1 teaspoon cornflour
1 tablespoon water

* If chicken stock is not available use a chicken
bouillon cube and water.

Use only the tender parts of the asparagus spears.
Cut each diagonally into 1-inch lengths. Place in
a pan with enough chicken stock to cover; put on
the lid and boil for 7-8 minutes. Cut the chicken

Chicken with asparagus

Sliced white chicken

breast into thin strips. Heat the oil till very hot. Add the chicken and fry for 2-3 minutes, tossing and shaking the pieces to cook them on all sides. Add the sherry, stock, soy sauce and seasonings and bring to the boil. Stir in the cornflour, blended with the water, and cook for 1½ minutes. Turn the well drained asparagus into a heated dish and pour the chicken and sauce over them.

BARK CHAM GAI
WHITE CUT CHICKEN

Preparation time   few minutes
Cooking time   1 hour 20 minutes - 1½ hours
To serve   8-10

You will need

1 5½-6 lb. fat capon
salt
½ oz. fresh ginger, crushed

Have ready a pot of slightly salted boiling water, enough to cover the bird. Lower the cleaned capon into it, put on the lid and bring to the boil again. Lift out the bird by inserting the handle of a wooden spoon into the vent and drain the liquid back into the pot.
Sprinkle the inside of the bird with salt and place half the crushed ginger in it. Drop the rest of the ginger into the pot and return the bird to it. Cover, bring to the boil again and simmer for 5 minutes. Remove the pot from the heat and leave it, covered, for 1 hour when the bird will be just warm.
Carve the capon into suitable pieces and coat them with the garlic sauce if used.

SOON HONG YAU
GARLIC SAUCE

Preparation time   1-2 minutes
Cooking time   none

You will need

up to 1 bulb garlic
2 tablespoons fat (see below)
stock from white cut chicken (see above)
salt to taste
1 teaspoon soy sauce
Very finely chop the garlic.
Pound into it the hot fat skimmed from the white cut chicken stock and enough of the hot stock itself to make a sauce the consistency of thin cream.
Add the salt and soy sauce.

BARK CHAM GAI HUNG
SLICED WHITE CHICKEN

No preparation
No cooking
To serve   2-3

This is another way of presenting Bark Cham Gai (white cut chicken see above).
Simply cut 4-6 slices of chicken.
Place them on a serving dish and garnish them with parsley or watercress.

GAI SEE NGAR CHOY

CHICKEN BREASTS WITH BEAN SPROUTS

Preparation time 4-5 minutes
Cooking time 7-8 minutes
To serve 2

You will need

8 oz. bean sprouts (see page 102)
3 tablespoons cooked chicken, in strips
2 tablespoons peanut oil
1 small onion, roughly chopped
chicken stock
pepper, salt, Ve-Tsin (see page 151)
1 teaspoon ginger sherry (see page 151)
¾ teaspoon soy sauce
1 teaspoon cornflour
1 dessertspoon water

Pick over sprouts, discarding any seeds. Heat half oil and quickly fry onion in it. Add 1 teaspoon chicken stock, tiny pinch pepper, good pinch salt and pinch Ve-Tsin and sprouts and cook for 3 minutes, turning sprouts over and over. Transfer to a heated dish; keep hot. Wipe out pan. Add remaining oil; toss and cook the chicken pieces in it at a good heat for 1 minute. Add ¼ pint (U.S. ⅝ cup) chicken stock, sherry, seasonings and soy sauce. Stir in cornflour, blended with the water, and cook for a further 1½ minutes. Put on bean sprouts. Serve.

Chicken breasts with bean sprouts

Deep-fat fried chicken

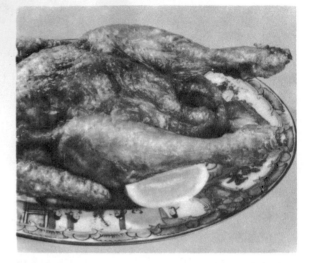

CHAR JEE GAI

DEEP-FAT FRIED CHICKEN

Preparation time 5 minutes
Cooking time 15-18 minutes
To serve 6-8

You will need

1 3-3¼-lb. roasting chicken
¾ teaspoon salt
good pinch each pepper and Ve-Tsin
   (see page 151)
peanut oil
lemon crescents

Ask the poulterer to draw and clean the bird but leave it untrussed.
Mix the salt, pepper and Ve-Tsin together and very thoroughly sprinkle the inside and outside of the bird with them, rubbing the mixture well in.
In a pan wide enough and deep enough for the chicken, place enough oil to half submerge the bird. Heat it to approximately 350°F. or 176°C. or to the stage when a slice of raw potato or onion dropped into it rests for a few seconds then rises to the surface. The Chinese cook places the chicken, breast down, on a flat skimmer, lowers it into the hot oil and fries it for 15-18 minutes, gradually turning it as it fries so that it is evenly browned all over.
The chicken is drained by inserting the handle of a spoon in the vent and up-ending the bird.
Place the chicken on a heated platter and garnish it with lemon crescents.
This is one of the few finished dishes which needs to be carved. As the chicken is not trussed, the heat

62

can get at all parts of it, including the difficult joints, so that it is properly cooked and unbelievably moist.

MOW GOO GAI KOW

CHICKEN WITH WHITE BUTTON MUSHROOMS

Preparation time   10 minutes
Cooking time   about 10 minutes
To serve   2-3

You will need

1 small onion
2 oz. cultivated button mushrooms
3 tablespoons raw dark chicken meat
1 tablespoon peanut oil
½ teaspoon ginger sherry (see page 151)
¼ pint (U.S. ⅝ cup) chicken stock
pinch each salt, sugar and Ve-Tsin
   (see page 151)
½ teaspoon soy sauce
1 teaspoon cornflour
1 dessertspoon cold water

Roughly chop the onion and quarter the mushrooms. After removing all tendons, cut the chicken meat into pieces the size of a largish butter bean. Heat the oil in a frying-pan. Cook the onion for 2 minutes at a high heat. Add and fry the chicken

Chicken with white button mushrooms

pieces for 3-4 minutes. Add the mushrooms and cook them for 1 minute.
Sprinkle in the sherry, stock, seasonings and soy sauce and cook for 1 minute.
Stir in the cornflour, blended with the water, bring to the boil and simmer for 1½ minutes.

GONG BO GAI DENG

CHICKEN WITH GREEN PEPPER

Preparation time   5-6 minutes
Cooking time   4-6 minutes
To serve   2-3

You will need

2-3 tablespoons raw dark chicken
   meat (leg)
salt, sugar and Ve-Tsin (see page 151)
1 teaspoon cornflour
3 teaspoons water
2-3 tablespoons green sweet pepper
2 tablespoons canned bamboo shoots
1 chopped onion
1 crushed clove garlic
peanut oil
¼ teaspoon ginger sherry (see page 151)
few drops sesame oil
few shakes pepper
½ teaspoon soy sauce
4-5 tablespoons hot chicken stock

Dice the chicken. Work in a tiny pinch salt, sugar, Ve-Tsin, ½ teaspoon cornflour and teaspoon water. Place ready. Dice the green pepper (not too finely) and the bamboo shoots and have them ready, each separate from the chicken and themselves. Heat enough oil for deep frying. Separately heat 1 tablespoon oil and fry the onion and garlic in it until the onion is golden. Discard the garlic. Add the sweet pepper and cook for 1 minute. Add the bamboo shoots, sherry, sesame oil, a further pinch salt, sugar and Ve-Tsin, soy sauce and chicken stock. Boil hard for 2 minutes. Meanwhile, when the deep oil has reached a temperature of 375°F. or 190°C., add the chicken pieces and fry them all a golden colour. Lift out, drain well and add to the vegetables. Finally, blend the remaining cornflour with the rest of the water, add it and boil for 1½ minutes. Turn all into a heated dish and serve.

GAI SEE JAR MIN
CHICKEN WITH BEAN SPROUTS AND CRISPY NOODLES

(Illustrated in colour on page 75)

Preparation time (apart from the noodles)
                    4-5 minutes
Cooking time   6-7 minutes
To serve   2-3

You will need

1 noodle 'nest' (see page 116)
1 tablespoon peanut oil
1 slice onion
2 tablespoons bean sprouts
2 tablespoons thin strips cooked chicken breast
pinch each salt, sugar and Ve-Tsin
    (see page 151)
¼ teaspoon soy sauce
¼ teaspoon ginger sherry (see page 151)
½ teaspoon sesame oil
4 tablespoons chicken stock
¾ teaspoon cornflour
1 tablespoon water
few extra strips cooked chicken breast
    (for garnish)

Lower the noodle 'nest' into hot oil for its first immersion, as directed on page 116. Lift out, drain and set aside for the final operation.
Heat the oil in a frying-pan. Cut the slice of onion into strips and add them. Cook for 1 minute. Add the bean sprouts and cook for a further minute. Add the chicken, seasonings, soy sauce, sherry, sesame oil and chicken stock and make really hot, tossing the ingredients about. Add the cornflour, blended with the water, and cook for 1½ minutes. Turn into a heated serving dish.
Reheat the deep oil to 365°-375°F. or 185°-190°C. Lower the basket containing the noodle 'nest' into it and leave just long enough to crisp the noodles to a deep warm cream colour. Place on top of the savoury mixture. Serve with watercress and three sauces — chilli, mustard and plum (see pages 8 and 15).

Note

If you can buy noodles cooked to the preliminary stage and ready for the second immersion in the hot oil, the time of preparation will be much lessened.

Chicken with green peas

CHENG DOW GAI DING
CHICKEN WITH GREEN PEAS

Preparation time 10 minutes
Cooking time   5-6 minutes
To serve   2

You will need

3 tablespoons chicken breast
3 tablespoons barely cooked peas
1 tablespoon peanut oil
1 sliced small onion
¼ teaspoon ginger sherry (see page 151)
¼ pint (U.S. ⅝ cup) chicken stock
small pinch each salt, sugar and Ve-Tsin
    (see page 151)
½ teaspoon soy sauce
1 level teaspoon cornflour
1 dessertspoon water

Cut the chicken into pieces the size of butter beans. Have ready the barely cooked peas. (If they are frozen, they need only be defrosted.)
Heat the oil in a frying-pan and for 1 minute quickly cook the onion in it.
Add and cook the chicken pieces for ½ minute. Next, add the sherry, stock, seasonings, soy sauce and peas and cook all together for 3-4 minutes. Stir in the cornflour, blended with the water, and keep the mixture moving while it cooks for a further 1½ minutes.

HUNG YEN GAI
CHICKEN AND ALMONDS

Preparation time 10 minutes
Cooking time 8-9 minutes
To serve 2

You will need

2 tablespoons raw breast of chicken
2 tablespoons roasted almonds
peanut oil
1 tablespoon canned bamboo shoots
1 tablespoon canned water chestnuts
1 tablespoon unpeeled cucumber
1 chopped small onion
¼ pint (U.S. ⅝ cup) chicken stock
½ teaspoon ginger sherry (see page 151)
pinch each salt, sugar and Ve-Tsin
   (see page 151)
½ teaspoon soy sauce
½-¾ teaspoon cornflour
1 dessertspoon water

Cut the chicken into smallish pieces, about half as large again as an almond. Blanch the almonds by dropping them into boiling water for 2 minutes, then into cold water. Slip off the skins by pinching one end of each almond. Dry the almonds, coat them with a little peanut oil and either place them in a tin and bake them to a warm gold in the oven at 400°F. or Gas Mark 6 or place them in a frying-pan and toss and stir them over a fair heat. (The

Chicken and almonds

oven method results in a more uniform colour.) Thinly slice the bamboo shoots and thickly slice the water chestnuts. Dice the cucumber and roughly chop the onion. Heat 2 tablespoons peanut oil and fry the onion in it for 1 minute. Add the chicken and cook for 2 minutes at high heat. Add the other vegetables and cook for 2 minutes. Add the stock, seasonings and soy sauce and cook for 1 minute. Stir in the cornflour, blended with the water, bring to the boil and cook for 1½ minutes. Turn into a heated dish and serve with plain boiled rice.

DOW SEE NGAP
DUCK WITH BLACK BEANS

Preparation time 7-8 minutes
Cooking time 5-6 minutes
To serve 2-3

You will need

4 tablespoons roast duck
salt, sugar and Ve-Tsin (see page 151)
1 teaspoon ginger sherry (see page 151)
few drops sesame oil
1 teaspoon soy sauce
pinch cornflour
2-3 thin slices fresh ginger
1 clove garlic
1 tablespoon canned black beans
peanut oil
1 small onion, chopped
1 small ladle hot chicken stock
1 level teaspoon cornflour
1 dessertspoon water

Cut the duck into suitable mouth-sized pieces. Turn them into a bowl. Add a pinch salt, sugar, Ve-Tsin, ½ teaspoon ginger sherry, few drops sesame oil, ½ teaspoon soy sauce and pinch cornflour and work them well into the meat. Chop the ginger and garlic very finely, add them to black beans, mash them together and work into a smooth paste. Heat 1 table-spoon oil in a frying-pan and cook the onion in it for 1-2 minutes. Add the black bean paste mixture and cook for a further minute. Add the duck with a little extra oil, if necessary, and toss it about while it heats through. Add the hot stock and a further pinch salt, sugar, Ve-Tsin, remaining ginger sherry, few drops sesame oil and rest of the soy sauce. Blend the cornflour with the water and stir it into the boiling mixture. Cook for a further 1½ minutes.

Stuffed chicken wings

LUNG CHIN FONG YICK
STUFFED CHICKEN WINGS

Preparation time 6-8 minutes
Cooking time 2-3 minutes
To serve 2-3

You will need

2 middle joints of chicken wings (white cut
  chicken see page 61)
2 strips cooked ham
2 strips raw carrot
2 strips raw Pacific prawn
salt and pepper
little beaten egg
1 teaspoon self-raising flour
peanut oil
4 tablespoons chicken stock
few drops soy sauce
few drops ginger sherry (see page 151)
pinch Ve-Tsin (see page 151)
½ teaspoon cornflour
1 teaspoon water
parsley sprigs

The wings are taken from the white cut chicken.
The middle joints are held firmly in one hand and
gently turned and twisted with the thumb and forefinger of the other so that the bones can be removed
easily.
Fill each bone cavity with a thin strip each of the
ham, carrot and prawn. Season with salt and
pepper, then dip in the beaten egg and then the
flour. Deep fat fry them in the very hot oil for 1-1½
minutes. Meanwhile, make the sauce. Put the stock

in a small pan, add the soy sauce, sherry, pinch of
salt and pinch of Ve-Tsin and bring to the boil.
Blend the cornflour with the water and stir it into
the well-flavoured stock. Cut the stuffed wings into
pieces and place them in a heated serving dish.
Spoon the sauce over them and garnish with the
parsley sprigs.

SHIU NGAP
ROAST DUCK

Preparation time 20-25 minutes if the duck is
  already drawn
Cooking time 1 hour
To serve up to 7 people (see note below)

You will need

1 5-6 lb. domestic duck
1 tablespoon ginger sherry (see page 151)
salt
½ teaspoon Ve-Tsin (see page 151)
1 teaspoon finely chopped fresh ginger
1 finely chopped spring onion
2-3 tablespoons golden syrup

Ask the poulterer to draw the duck in such a way
that the openings at each end are as small as
possible, because, later on, they have to be closed.
Chop off the wing tips.
Mix together the sherry, 1 teaspoon salt, Ve-Tsin,
ginger and onion and have them ready. Stand the
can of syrup in a pan of warm water to melt it
slightly and make it more liquid.
Rub the inside of the duck with the sherry mixture,
then seal both the neck and body ends very well.
Rub salt all over into the surface. Work the skin
away from the ends of the wings where the tips
were cut off. Insert a thin plastic tube into each
and blow into it to encourage the skin to separate
from the flesh. Secure both ends. You now have
a perfectly sealed inflated duck.
Lay the duck breast down and generously brush all
reachable surface with the syrup. Turn the bird
over and give the other side the same treatment.
Impale the duck on a stout skewer at the tail end.
Wrap oiled greaseproof paper over the other end to
protect it from too much heat during the cooking. In
an oven preheated to 400°F. or Gas Mark 6, place
a runner fairly high but allow for ease in slipping
the skewer across the bars so that the duck will hang
down. Have a baking tray beneath the duck.
Bake for 1 hour, when the bird should be crisp
and golden. This duck can be eaten hot or cold.
Here is how to serve it.

First, cut off the wings and legs and chop them across into mouth-sized pieces with a chopper or strong sharp knife. Carve the meat from the body in thin diagonal slices, making sure that a portion of skin remains on each.

Note

This duck will be enough for up to 7 servings if other meats are served at the same meal. If duck alone is to be served, there will be sufficient portions for 4-5 persons.

BAT FAR GAI

'WHITE FLOWER' CHICKEN

Preparation time 8-10 minutes
Cooking time 5 minutes
To serve 2-3

You will need

1 large raw skinned breast of roasting chicken
few drops ginger sherry (see page 151)
salt and Ve-Tsin (see page 151)
few shakes pepper
3 raw Pacific prawns
3 canned water chestnuts
1 small spring onion
1 small egg white
few drops sesame oil
½-1 level teaspoon cornflour
peanut oil

Cut the skinned chicken breast diagonally into 3 slices so that each is as large as possible. Work the sherry, pinch salt, pinch Ve-Tsin and a few shakes pepper into them and set aside.

Remove the shells and the black intestinal lines, then chop the prawns, chestnuts and onion and mix to a smooth paste. Beat the egg white to a slight froth and work it in, together with a further pinch salt, pinch Ve-Tsin, few shakes pepper and the sesame oil.

Lay the chicken slices on a clean surface (an enamelled tray is ideal) and sprinkle them with the cornflour. Place a portion of the prawn paste on each and smooth it to the shape of the slice but slightly rounded on top.

Heat the oil to 375°F. or 190°C. Drop the chicken slices into it and cook them for 5 minutes. Lift out and cut into diagonal slices. Slip the knife under each and carefully transfer to a heated serving dish so that each portion retains its shape.

Chicken with oyster sauce

HOI YOW GAI KOW

CHICKEN WITH OYSTER SAUCE

Preparation time 5-6 minutes
Cooking time 4 minutes
To serve 2

You will need

4 oz. raw chicken breast
2 teaspoons cornflour
1 tablespoon water
1 dessertspoon peanut oil
¼ pint (U.S. ⅝ cup) chicken stock
pinch each salt and sugar
good pinch Ve-Tsin (see page 151)
½ teaspoon ginger sherry (see page 151)
1 dessertspoon oyster sauce
parsley

Cut the chicken breast into very thin slices. The best way to do this is to place the meat on a board then, holding it firmly with one hand, slice it with the other.

Blend the cornflour with the water and work half into the pieces of chicken. Set aside for a minute or so.

Heat the oil till very hot. Fry the chicken pieces in it for 1½-2 minutes, stirring and tossing them as they cook.

Add the stock, seasonings, sherry, remaining cornflour mixture and oyster sauce. Bring to a good boil and simmer for 1½ minutes. Turn into a heated dish and garnish with parsley.

BOR LOW GNAP
DUCK WITH PINEAPPLE

Preparation time 5 minutes
Cooking time 7-8 minutes
To serve 2-3

You will need

3 tablespoons raw duck leg meat
2 teaspoons cornflour
1 tablespoon water
3 tablespoons canned pineapple
2 tablespoons peanut oil
1-2 teaspoons ginger sherry*
¼ pint (U.S. ⅝ cup) chicken stock
pinch each salt, sugar and Ve-Tsin
  (see page 151)
½ teaspoon soy sauce

* Cut 2 oz. fresh ginger into thin strips. Turn the strips into a bottle, cover with half bottle warm brown sherry, leave to infuse, strain and use as directed.

Cut the meat into butter bean-sized pieces. Blend together the cornflour and water. Thoroughly work a third of the mixture into the meat and set aside for 1-2 minutes. Cut the pineapple into pieces similar sized to the meat.
Very well heat 1 tablespoon oil in a frying-pan. Fry the pieces of pineapple in it for 1 minute, stirring and tossing them as they cook. Turn into a heated dish and keep hot. Wipe out the pan. Heat the

Duck with pineapple

remaining oil in it, add the meat and cook for 4 minutes, stirring and tossing to cook it evenly. Add the sherry, seasonings and soy sauce and cook rapidly for 1 minute. Stir in the remaining cornflour liquid, bring to the boil and simmer for 1½ minutes. Lastly, return the pineapple to the pan and heat through.

BAT BOW CHIN NGAP
BONED DUCK, CANTONESE STYLE

(Illustrated in colour on page 58)
Preparation time 20-30 minutes
Cooking time 2½-3 hours
To serve 6-7

You will need

1 5-5½ lb. duck
peanut oil
4 tablespoons lean raw pork, cut in thin strips
salt, sugar and Ve-Tsin (see page 151)
soy sauce
4 tablespoons canned water chestnuts
1 fairly large spring onion, cut in 1½-inch lengths
6 tablespoons shelled ordinary chestnuts
1 scant dessertspoon ginger sherry
  (see above)
4-5 tablespoons chicken stock
3 tablespoons lotus nuts
3 tablespoons sliced lean roast pork
3 tablespoons sliced canned
  bamboo shoots
3 tablespoons sliced canned awabi
1 teaspoon sesame oil

GARNISH

4-5 Chinese mushrooms (see page 150)
carrots
oil
lettuce heart leaves
mustard and cress or watercress or other salad
  vegetable available

Ask the poulterer to draw the bird through the neck end, to make the smallest possible cut at the vent and to bone it without breaking the skin. (This is not difficult for a first-class poulterer.) The boned duck must be 'water-tight' before being cooked.
Place the prepared ingredients, side by side, on a large platter, with the cooked pork apart from the others.

Heat a tablespoon of the oil and fry the raw pork in it for a minute, moving the pieces about in the pan. Add a very tiny pinch each of salt, sugar and Ve-Tsin and ½ teaspoon soy sauce. Continue to cook for 3 minutes, tossing the pieces.

Transfer them to a plate.

Wipe out the pan.

Add another tablespoon of oil and cook the water chestnuts and spring onions in it for a minute. Add the ordinary chestnuts, sherry, stock and lotus nuts and toss the mixture over a good heat. Again add a pinch each of the three seasonings, then add the roast pork, bamboo shoots and awabi and continue to cook for ½ minute. Add the sesame oil and, if necessary, further seasonings and soy sauce. Do not overdo them.

This stuffing must be moist, so, if the moisture has evaporated, add a little hot water. (Further stock might make the stuffing too salty.)

Sew up the small opening at the vent, then lay the duck on the table and place the filling in it. Pack it loosely because some of the ingredients will go on swelling and this could cause the skin to break. Tie the neck end securely, turning the end over and tying it again.

Have a pan large enough to hold the duck in a flat position. Pour enough peanut oil into it to come one-third up the duck. Heat it to 350°-360°F. or 176°-182°C. Place the duck in a frying-basket or on a long-handled skimmer and lower it into the hot oil.

Baste the breast for 3 minutes with a large spoon. Remove and leave to become cold. This 'firming' process is to prevent the skin bursting. Return the duck to the hot oil and baste it until the breast is a warm golden brown.

Transfer it to a steamer with boiling water coming 1½ inches up it, cover tightly and steam for 2 hours. Remove the duck, let it settle for a few minutes, then remove the string and serve as below.

Meanwhile prepare the garnish.

Have ready the Chinese mushrooms and boil for 6 minutes in chicken stock. Drain them well. Cut thinly sliced carrots into fancy shapes or nick the edges all round with a knife. Cook them in oil without browning them.

Place the duck on a heated serving dish and garnish it with the mushrooms, carrots, heart leaves of lettuce, mustard and cress or watercress or other salad vegetable available.

Note

The above dish is possible only if the duck is boned without the skin being cut. Otherwise, it would not hold the stuffing when immersed in the hot oil.

Sweet-sour chicken

DIM SIN GAI
SWEET-SOUR CHICKEN

Preparation time 2-3 minutes
Cooking time 5-6 minutes
To serve 2-3

You will need

1 cooked breast of chicken
¼ pint (U.S. ⅝ cup) chicken stock
4 tablespoons water
½ small clove garlic, crushed
1 teaspoon peanut oil
¾ teaspoon sugar
¼ tablespoon tomato purée
4 tablespoons vinegar
pinch salt
½ teaspoon cornflour
1 teaspoon water
Chinese pickles for garnish (see page 140)

Take the breast from the cooked white cut chicken (see page 61). Add it to the heated stock and leave it for 2-3 minutes at just under boiling point. In a small pan, mix together the water, garlic, oil, sugar, tomato purée, vinegar and salt. Whisk while you bring them to the boil. Blend the cornflour with the water and stir it in. Simmer for 1½-2 minutes to complete the sweet-sour sauce. Drop in Chinese pickles to heat.

Lift out the chicken, cut it into mouth-sized pieces and place them in a heated serving dish. Strain the hot sauce over them, garnish with the pickles and serve.

YIM KOK GAI
SALT-BAKED CHICKEN

Preparation time up to 10 minutes
Cooking time 50 minutes-1 hour
To serve 5-6

You will need

1 2¾-3 lb. young roasting chicken (undrawn)
cooking salt
2-3 thin slices fresh ginger
1 spring onion
tiny pinch each salt and Ve-Tsin (see page 151)
1 teaspoon brandy

For this dish, you will need a casserole in which the chicken will not be lost but in which there is enough room for the hot salt below, around and above the bird. An enamelled iron casserole is ideal, because it heats well and retains the heat, but a strong earthenware one will do.

Let the casserole be heating gently in the oven and the coarse kitchen salt in a wide stout pan on top of the cooker. There should be enough salt to encase the bird completely in due course. Stir the salt to heat it evenly.

Draw and clean the chicken. Very finely chop the ginger and onion. Add the seasonings and brandy and work the mixture well into the inside of the chicken. Wrap it in strong greaseproof paper so that the juices, if any, are retained.

By this time, the cooking salt should be very hot. Spoon enough of it into the heated casserole to cover the bottom to a depth of ½-inch (¾-inch would be better; it depends on the depth of the casserole). Lay the wrapped bird, breast downwards, on top. Trickle in hot salt to surround the chicken on all sides and top with salt to a depth of ½-inch. Put on the lid and leave for 5 minutes.

Remove the chicken, reheat the salt and repeat the process four times — that is, five time in all. Remove the chicken. Cut off the wings and legs and chop them across into mouth-sized pieces. Carve the breast diagonally into similar sized pieces, retaining the skin, and serve.

Note

This is a very old way of preparing chicken and well worth the slight work involved.

Salt-baked chicken is possible even when there is only an electric hotplate or gas ring as the cooking equipment. One could serve boiled or fried rice with the chicken because, while it is cooking in the hot salt, the hotplate or ring is free.

A flame-proof earthenware or glass casserole could be used but it would be as well to have an asbestos mat between it and the heat. Incidentally, do not ever rest an earthenware or glass casserole on even a slightly damp surface.

JAR GAI PIN
CHICKEN BREASTS

Preparation time 3-4 minutes
Cooking time 2 minutes
To serve 2

You will need

2 raw chicken breasts
pinch salt
tiny pinch pepper
4 oz. self-raising flour
½ beaten egg
½ pint (U.S. 1¼ cups) water
peanut oil
lemon wedges

Trim the chicken breasts and rub the salt and pepper well into them. Dust them with a teaspoon of the flour and set them aside for the moment.

Make a batter by gradually adding the beaten egg and water to the remaining flour. In a deep pan heat enough oil in which to fry the breasts.

Dip them in the batter, drain and brown on both sides in the oil (about 2 minutes). Cut each piece

Chicken breasts

across into slices, arrange on a heated serving dish and garnish with the wedges of lemon.

GAI SEE CHOW MEIN

FRIED CHICKEN WITH NOODLES

Preparation time   30 minutes
Cooking time   8-9 minutes
To serve   3-4

You will need

¼ recipe egg noodles (see page 150)
peanut oil
4 tablespoons raw breast of chicken, shredded
1 medium-sized onion, cut in thin strips
1 shredded Chinese mushroom (see page 150)
4 oz. bean sprouts (picked over)
1 tablespoon canned bamboo shoots, shredded
¼ pint (U.S. ⅝ cup) chicken stock
pinch each salt, sugar and Ve-Tsin
   (see page 151)
½ teaspoon sesame oil
½ teaspoon ginger sherry (see page 151)
½ teaspoon soy sauce
¾ teaspoon cornflour
1 dessertspoon cold water
1 tablespoon boiled ham, shredded

Boil the noodles in plenty of water for 10 minutes. Drain well and sprinkle a few drops of peanut oil over them.
Heat 1 tablespoon peanut oil in a frying-pan and quickly cook the chicken strips in it for less than a minute, tossing and turning them all the time. Transfer them to a dish and keep them warm.
Add the onion to the pan, cook it for ¼ minute then add the mushroom and cook for a further ¾ minute, stirring them about. Now add the bean sprouts and bamboo shoots with, if necessary, a little more oil and cook for 2 minutes.
Next, add the stock, seasonings, sesame oil, sherry and soy sauce and cook for ½ minute. Blend the cornflour with the water and stir it in. Cook for 1½ minutes. Add the boiled noodles and ham and heat through.
Lastly add the chicken and stir all together for ¼ minute over a good heat.
Turn the mixture into a heated serving dish and sprinkle with the very finely shredded ham.

BOR LOW GAI

CHICKEN WITH PINEAPPLE

Preparation time   10 minutes
Cooking time   5 minutes
To serve   2

You will need

2 tablespoons raw chicken breast
3 oz. canned or fresh pineapple
2 dessertspoons peanut oil
1 small onion, roughly chopped
½ teaspoon ginger sherry (see page 151)
pinch each salt, sugar and Ve-Tsin
   (see page 151)
½ teaspoon soy sauce
4 tablespoons chicken stock
½ teaspoon cornflour
1 dessertspoon water

Cut chicken into thin slices. Drain pineapple. If in rings, cut into small wedges. If fresh cut a slice and remove peel; core and cut into small wedges. Heat half the oil in a frying-pan and fry pineapple and onion for 3 minutes. Remove and set aside.
Wipe out pan. Heat remaining oil in it. Add chicken pieces; toss and turn them for 3 minutes. Add sherry, seasonings, soy sauce and stock and bring to the boil. Return pineapple and onion to pan. Add cornflour, blended with water, and heat through for 1½ minutes.

Chicken with pineapple

HUNG YEN NGAP DING
DUCK WITH ALMONDS

Preparation time   10-15 minutes
Cooking time   5-6 minutes
To serve   3

You will need

1 small onion
2 tablespoons raw leg of duck
1 tablespoon canned bamboo shoots
1 tablespoon canned water chestnuts
1 tablespoon unpeeled cucumber
1 tablespoon canned pineapple
2 tablespoons almonds
1 tablespoon peanut oil
1 teaspoon ginger sherry (see page 151)
¼ pint (U.S. ⅝ cup) chicken stock
good pinch each salt, sugar and Ve-Tsin
  (see page 151)
½-1 teaspoon soy sauce
1 teaspoon cornflour
1 dessertspoon water

Roughly chop the onion. Cut the duck meat and bamboo shoots into strips. Slice the water chestnuts and dice the unpeeled cucumber and pineapple. Blanch and roast the almonds or brown them in a little hot peanut oil, moving them about to colour them evenly.
Heat the oil and fry the onion in it at a high heat for ¼ minute, stirring the pieces to cook them evenly.

Duck with almonds

Add the duck and stir for 1 minute. Add the sherry, stock and remaining vegetables, cook rapidly for 2 minutes then add the pineapple, seasonings and soy sauce with a little more stock, if necessary. Stir in the cornflour, blended with the water, and cook for 1½ minutes. Add the almonds, turn all into a heated dish and serve.

HAP TO NGAP
DUCK WITH WALNUTS

Preparation time   10 minutes
Cooking time   8-10 minutes
To serve   2-3

You will need

2 tablespoons shelled walnuts
2-3 tablespoons raw leg of duck
1 tablespoon unpeeled cucumber
1 tablespoon canned bamboo shoots
1 tablespoon canned water chestnuts
1 small chopped onion
2 tablespoons peanut oil
¼ pint (U.S. ⅝ cup) hot chicken stock
1 teaspoon ginger sherry (see page 151)
pinch each salt, sugar and Ve-Tsin
  (see page 151)
½ teaspoon soy sauce
1 level teaspoon cornflour
1 tablespoon water

Drop the shelled walnuts into boiling water for 1-2 minutes. Drain, peel, dry thoroughly and set aside.
Cut the duck leg diagonally into slices half as large again as the half walnuts.
Dice the cucumber, thinly slice the bamboo shoots and slice the chestnuts more thickly. Set each aside separately.
Heat the oil in a frying-pan. Lightly brown the walnuts in it then lift them out. Add the onion and cook for 1 minute, then add the duck and fry for 3 minutes at high heat, tossing and turning the pieces about.
Add the cucumber, bamboo shoots and chestnuts in that order and cook for 2 minutes. Add the stock, seasonings soy sauce and cook for 1 minute. Add the walnuts and heat through. Blend the cornflour with the water, stir it in and cook for 1½ minutes.
Turn into a heated dish and serve.

SUI LING GAI

STEAMED CHICKEN WITH VEGETABLE GARNISH

Preparation time   7-8 minutes
Cooking time   30 minutes
To serve   2

You will need

4 tablespoons sliced raw chicken breast
1¼ teaspoons cornflour
2 teaspoons water
few drops peanut oil
few drops ginger sherry (see page 151)
1 shredded Chinese mushroom (see page 150)
1 good teaspoon shredded Szechwan cabbage
   (see page 79)
¼ pint (U.S. ⅝ cup) chicken stock
few drops soy sauce
pinch each salt, sugar and Ve-Tsin
   (see page 151)
spring onion stalks

Place the chicken on a small plate. Blend ½ teaspoon cornflour and 1 teaspoon water. Put the mixture, oil and sherry on the chicken. Put the mushroom and cabbage on the chicken, place in a steamer and steam for 30 minutes.
Bring the stock, soy sauce and seasonings to the boil in a small pan. Stir in the remaining cornflour, blended with the rest of the water, and simmer for 1½—2 minutes.
Carefully remove the chicken on to a heated serving dish; pour the sauce over it and garnish with the green stalk of a spring onion.

Steamed chicken with vegetable garnish

DOW SEE GAI

CHICKEN AND BLACK BEANS

Preparation time   7-8 minutes
Cooking time   7-8 minutes
To serve   2-3

You will need

3 tablespoons raw dark chicken meat
salt, sugar and Ve-Tsin (see page 151)
1 teaspoon ginger sherry (see page 151)
sesame oil
1 teaspoon soy sauce
cornflour
2-3 thin slices fresh ginger
1 clove garlic
1 tablespoon canned black beans
peanut oil
1 small onion, chopped
1 small ladle chicken stock
1 dessertspoon water

Cut the chicken meat into slices and place them in a bowl. Add a pinch salt, sugar, Ve-Tsin, ½ teaspoon sherry, few drops sesame oil, ½ teaspoon soy sauce and a pinch cornflour and work all thoroughly together.
Leave to rest.
Chop the ginger and garlic. Add the black beans and mash together to a smooth paste. Heat 1 dessertspoon of peanut oil in frying-pan and cook the onion in it for 1-2 minutes. Add the above paste and cook for a further minute.
Meanwhile, have deep peanut oil heating to 375°F. or 190°C. Drop the chicken pieces into it and cook them till a warm gold colour. Drain them and add them to the frying-pan. Add also another pinch salt, sugar, Ve-Tsin, the remaining sherry, few drops sesame oil, remaining soy sauce and the stock. Bring to the boil.
Finally, blend 1 level teaspoon cornflour with the water, stir it in and boil for 1½ minutes.
Turn the mixture into a heated dish and serve at once.

MUI GEE GAI
SWEET PLUM CHICKEN

Preparation time 6-7 minutes
Cooking time 6-7 minutes
To serve 2-3

You will need

2-3 raw chicken breasts
2 crushed cloves garlic
1-2 teaspoons ginger sherry (see page 151)
pinch each salt and Ve-Tsin (see page 151)
2 shakes pepper
1 dessertspoon beaten egg
2-3 tablespoons self-raising flour
deep peanut oil

PLUM SAUCE

2 tablespoons canned plum sauce
  (see page 151)
3-4 tablespoons hot chicken stock
1 tablespoon dark sugar crystals*
1 tablespoon hot water

* These are like very dark coffee crystals.

Cut the chicken breasts into thinnish scallops about
3½ inches long. Add the garlic and then the sherry
and seasonings. Work them well into the chicken
pieces. Next, add the beaten egg and work it in too.
Discard the garlic. Dip the strips of chicken in the
flour and shake off excess. Work the flour well into
the chicken.
Meanwhile, have the oil heating to 375°F. or 190°C.
Drop the chicken pieces into it and cook to a golden
colour, separating the pieces during the cooking, if
necessary. Drain, place on a heated serving dish and
hand the hot sauce separately.

TO MAKE THE PLUM SAUCE

Blend together the canned plum sauce and stock.
Dissolve the sugar in the hot water and add it. Heat
together, then rub through a sieve.

GUNG PIN NGAP
GINGER DUCK

Preparation time 5-6 minutes (plus resting
  time)
Cooking time 6-8 minutes
To serve 2

You will need

4-5 tablespoons raw breast of duck
very tiny pinch bicarbonate of soda
15 very thin slices fresh ginger
2-3 young spring onions
good pinch each salt and Ve-Tsin
  (see page 151)
½ teaspoon sugar
several shakes pepper
3 teaspoons ginger sherry (see page 151)
2 tablespoons peanut oil
4 tablespoons hot chicken stock
1 good teaspoon cornflour
1 dessertspoon water

Place the skinned raw breast of duck on a board and
hold it in position with one hand while cutting it
diagonally into thin slices with the other.
Work the bicarbonate of soda into them and leave
to rest for at least 1 hour. (Duck is a firm meat. The
effect of the soda on it is to tenderise it.) Cut the
ginger into thin strips and the onions into 2-inch
lengths.
Work the seasonings and 2 teaspoons sherry into
the duck.
Heat the oil in a frying pan. Add the duck and toss
it while cooking for 3 minutes. Add the ginger and
onions and cook for another 2 minutes. Add the hot
stock and the remaining ginger sherry. Bring to the
boil.
Stir in the cornflour, blended with the water, and
boil for 1½ minutes.
Turn into a heated dish and serve.

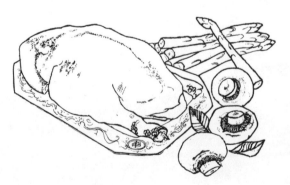

Chicken with bean sprouts and crispy noodles

Steamed meat in noodle cases

MEAT

YUK

The Chinese, when they can afford it, are great meateaters — great, that is, in the number of meat dishes they have but not great in the amount of meat there is in a dish.

Pork is the favourite meat and some of the most sought after Chinese dishes in the Western world are made of pork.

Such dishes, for instance, as pork meat balls, sweet-sour pork, barbecued spare ribs of pork, and roast belly of pork (see page 79), to mention only a few, have become so well known as almost to be considered Western ones.

Pork is succulent meat. Beef, though liked, is not so much used for economic reasons. It is expensive but, here again, 'a little goes a long way'. But the smaller amounts (to Western eyes) used in a dish are satisfactory and satisfying.

It will be noticed that, in most of the recipes in this section, chicken stock is given as an ingredient. Generally, only a few tablespoons of it are required. In the kitchen of a Chinese restaurant, whose menu contains so many chicken dishes, rich chicken stock is always available. In the home kitchen, however, this is not always possible. As an alternative, I suggest water and a chicken cube.

For home-made stock, another way is to buy giblets from a shop where cooked chickens are sold. I myself do this. The mixed giblets cost very little.

Reserve the chicken livers to be used by themselves. With the necks, hearts and gizzards, make the stock. When cold, turn it into a jar and 'bank' it in the refrigerator to be drawn on when needed.

SUI MAI

STEAMED MEAT IN NOODLE CASES

Preparation time	20-25 minutes (noodle dough)
	8-10 minutes (filling)
Cooking time	20 minutes
To serve	3-6

You will need

½ recipe noodle dough (see page 115)
6 oz. pork (a quarter in fat)
1 dessertspoon canned water chestnuts
1 dessertspoon canned bamboo shoots
pinch each salt, sugar and Ve-Tsin
  (see page 151)
1 teaspoon beaten egg
6 shelled cooked prawns

First, make the noodle dough. It is a good idea to do this early in the day. Put it into a basin, cover to prevent it drying and set aside while preparing the filling.

Very finely chop the pork, water chestnuts and bamboo shoots. Add the seasonings and work in the egg. Pick up the mixture and drop it on the table time and again so that the ingredients are well combined. Roll out the noodle dough very thinly and cut it into six 3-inch squares. Place a portion of the filling in the centre of each and form into cylindrical shapes. Pull out the top of each a little to make appear as a 'flower'. Place upright in a steamer, top each with a prawn, cover and steam for 20 minutes.

Note

If there are several dishes at the one course, as is the Chinese custom, this one would serve 6.

Rump steak with bean sprouts

NGOW YUK NGAR CHOY
RUMP STEAK
WITH BEAN SPROUTS

Preparation time 7-8 minutes
Cooking time 6-7 minutes
To serve 3-4

You will need

4 oz. bean sprouts
1 finely chopped clove garlic
4 oz. rump steak
salt, sugar and Ve-Tsin (see page 151)
tiny pinch pepper
9 teaspoons peanut oil
$\frac{1}{2}$ teaspoon soy sauce
$1\frac{1}{4}$ teaspoons cornflour
2 teaspoons cold water
1 crushed clove garlic
$\frac{1}{4}$ pint (U.S. $\frac{5}{8}$ cup) hot chicken stock
$\frac{1}{2}$ teaspoon ginger sherry (see page 151)
sprigs parsley

Pick over the bean sprouts and discard any seeds. Add the chopped garlic to the sprouts. Cut the rump steak into thin slices and then thin strips. Place the meat in a basin with a pinch of salt, sugar, Ve-Tsin and pepper and 1 teaspoon of peanut oil, soy sauce and $\frac{1}{2}$ teaspoon cornflour, blended with 1 teaspoon water. Work well together.
Heat 4 teaspoons of the oil and fry the bean sprouts in it for 1-$1\frac{1}{2}$ minutes, turning and tossing them about. Transfer the sprouts to a heated dish and keep hot. Wipe out the pan and get the remaining oil very hot in it. Fry the crushed clove of garlic in it until a golden colour and then discard the garlic. Add the prepared steak and cook it for 1-$1\frac{1}{2}$ minutes at high heat. Remove it.
Add to the pan the stock, sherry and pinch of salt, sugar and Ve-Tsin. Bring to the boil. Stir in the remaining cornflour, blended with the rest of the water, and boil for $1\frac{1}{2}$ minutes.
Return the steak to the pan and heat through. Add the bean sprouts. Turn all into a heated dish; garnish with parsley and serve.

CHAR GEE NGOW YUK
ESCALOPES OF RUMP STEAK

Preparation time 10 minutes
Cooking time 1-2 minutes
To serve 3-4

You will need

4 oz. rump steak
pinch each salt, sugar and Ve-Tsin
  (see page 151)
tiny pinch pepper
1 teaspoon beaten egg
$\frac{1}{2}$ teaspoon cornflour
1 teaspoon cold water
1 rounded tablespoon self-raising flour
peanut oil for deep frying
2 tablespoons Chinese pickle (see page 140)
1 tomato, quartered

SWEET-SOUR SAUCE

1 dessertspoon sugar
tiny pinch each salt, pepper and Ve-Tsin
1 dessertspoon malt vinegar
$\frac{1}{2}$ teaspoon tomato ketchup
$\frac{1}{2}$ teaspoon soy sauce
4 tablespoons water
$\frac{1}{2}$ teaspoon cornflour
1 dessertspoon cold water

First make the sweet-sour sauce. Mix together the first 6 ingredients. Bring them to the boil. Stir in the cornflour, blended with the water and boil for 2 minutes, stirring continuously.
Cut the rump steak into 2-inch strips, 4-5 inches long.
Put them into a basin with the seasonings, egg and cornflour blended with the water. Work them well into it and leave for a few minutes. Lift out and drop into the self-raising flour. Have the oil quite hot (355-360°F. or 180-182°C.). Cook the meat in it for $\frac{1}{2}$ minute, then raise the temperature to

Escalopes of rump steak

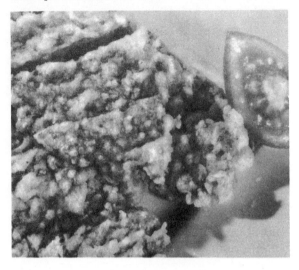

brown it. Meanwhile, add the pickle to the hot sauce. Turn it into a heated dish, place the rump steak on top and garnish with the quartered tomato.

NG HEUNG SHIU YUK
ROAST BELLY OF PORK

(Illustrated in colour on page 86)

Preparation time   10 minutes
Cooking time   45-50 minutes
To serve   10-14

You will need

2-2½ lb. belly of fresh pork (boned)
coarse salt
1 tablespoon soy bean (see page 151)
1-2 pinches salt
1-2 good pinches sugar
good pinch Ve-Tsin (see page 151)
1 finely chopped clove garlic
2 finely chopped thin slices fresh ginger
  (see page 151)
watercress, heart of letttuce, tomatoes
onion 'flowers' (see page 49)

Lay the pork, skin side up, on a board and pierce it all over with a fork. Rub coarse salt into the pork on both sides.
Mash together the soy bean, seasonings, garlic and ginger to a paste. Rub it into the boned side of the meat.
Pass a long metal skewer, lengthwise, through the pork to keep it in position during the cooking.

Attach two hooks to the meat and hang it on the top runner of the oven, with the baking tin beneath it. Cook for 20 minutes at 475°F. or Gas Mark 9. Unhook the meat and transfer it to the baking tin. Cook for a further 30-40 minutes. Leave to become cold.
Cut into long slices and then mouth-sized pieces and serve, as illustrated, garnished with the vegetables and onion 'flowers'.

Note

This cut of pork is one of the most delicious and inexpensive of all meats. With other dishes at the meal, it will serve 10-14 people or last the family several days.

JAR CHOY GING CEE YUK
STEAMED PORK WITH SALT CABBAGE (SZECHWAN)

Preparation time   10 minutes
Cooking time   8 minutes
To serve   2-3

You will need

3 tablespoons Chinese salt cabbage
1 teaspoon sugar
4 tablespoons raw leg of pork
pinch each salt and Ve-Tsin (see page 151)
1ew shakes pepper
1 teaspoon ginger sherry (see page 151)
few drops sesame oil
1 chopped clove garlic
1 chopped thin slice fresh ginger
1 teaspoon soy sauce
1 good teaspoon pork dripping
1 teaspoon chopped spring onion

Well cover the cabbage with cold water. Bring to the boil and boil for 2-3 minutes. Drain, rinse in cold water, drain again and squeeze out moisture. Add the sugar and work it well in.
Cut the pork into very thin slices. Put them into a basin and add the seasonings, sherry, sesame oil, garlic, ginger and soy sauce.
Mix all well together and finally add and work in the pork dripping.
Place the mixture on an oiled plate, cover with greaseproof paper and steam for 8 minutes.
Cut into slices and sprinkle with the onion which should include both the white and green.

CHEN GWAR CHOW YUK PIN
PORK WITH CUCUMBER

Preparation time   7-8 minutes
Cooking time   8-9 minutes
To serve   3

You will need

4 oz. lean pork
salt
sugar
Ve-Tsin (see page 151)
1 teaspoon peanut oil
scant 1½ teaspoons cornflour
2 teaspoons water
1 small onion
1 7-8 inches long cucumber
1 tablespoon pork dripping
1 crushed clove garlic
½ teaspoon ginger sherry (see page 151)
¼ pint (U.S. ⅝ cup) chicken stock
¼ teaspoon soy sauce

Cut the pork across the grain into thin slices. Place the slices in a bowl, add a pinch of salt, sugar and Ve-Tsin, the oil, 1 scant teaspoon cornflour and 1 teaspoon water, and work them well into them. Cut the onion into 4 pieces. Quarter the cucumber full length then slice it diagonally across into 2-inch lengths.
Melt half the dripping in a frying-pan. Cook the

Pork with cucumber

garlic in it till pale golden and then discard it. Fry the pork into the hot dripping for 4 minutes. Sprinkle it with the sherry then transfer the meat to a dish.
Wipe out the pan. Add the remaining dripping. Toss the vegetables in it for 1 minute. Add another pinch salt, sugar and Ve-Tsin and the soy sauce and cook for 3 minutes. Stir in the remaining cornflour, blended with the rest of the water, and boil up for 1½ minutes. Add the pork and heat through.
Turn all on to a heated dish and serve.

SUNG TUNG
NGOW CHAI YUK
FILLET OF VEAL
WITH MUSHROOMS

Preparation time   6-8 minutes
Cooking time   5-6 minutes
To serve   2-3

You will need

3 oz. fillet of veal in one piece
½ small beaten egg
½ teaspoon soy sauce
pinch salt
few shakes pepper
1 tablespoon peanut oil
2 tablespoons diced (not too small) canned
   bamboo shoots
2 tablespoons thinly sliced unopened button
   mushrooms
pinch Ve-Tsin (see page 151)
3-4 tablespoons hot chicken stock
½ teaspoon cornflour
1 dessertspoon water

Cut the veal diagonally into very thin slices and work the egg, soy sauce, salt and pepper into them. Heat the oil in a frying-pan. Add the veal and fry it for 2 minutes at a high heat. Transfer it to a heated serving dish and keep it hot.
Quickly fry the bamboo shoots and mushrooms for 1 minute at the same high heat. Add the Ve-Tsin and stock and cook for 1 minute. Blend the cornflour with the water, stir it in and boil for 1½ minutes.
Turn this vegetable mixture and its sauce over the veal and serve at once.

Steamed pork

Roast lean pork

JING GEE YUK BENG
STEAMED PORK

Preparation time　15-20 minutes
Cooking time　15 minutes
To serve　3-4

You will need

6 oz. lean pork
1 dessertspoon spring onion
1 teaspoon soy sauce
1 dessertspoon cornflour
pinch salt
pinch sugar
small pinch pepper
pinch Ve-Tsin (see page 151)
1 onion 'flower' (see page 49)
parsley

Finely chop the meat and onion. (Chinese cooks do this with two knives.)
Work in the remaining ingredients, except the onion 'flower' and parsley garnish. Knead very well with the heel of the hand and throw the mixture on to the board over and over again.
Knead into an oval shape and place it on a plate which has been lightly rubbed with a little peanut oil.
Put it in a steamer, cover tightly and steam for 15 minutes.
Slice it on to a heated serving dish and garnish with the onion 'flower' and parsley.

CHAR SHIU
ROAST LEAN PORK

Preparation time　10 minutes
Cooking time　30 minutes
To serve　3-4

You will need

12 oz. lean leg of pork
pinch salt
pinch sugar
pinch Ve-Tsin (see page 151)
few drops cochineal
1 dessertspoon red soya bean curd
1 dessertspoon soy sauce
parsley

Have the pork cut the way of the grain. Divide it, lengthwise, into two strips. Place them in a bowl. Add the salt, sugar, Ve-Tsin, cochineal, bean curd and soy sauce.
Work these well together until the meat soaks them up.
Impale each piece of meat on a wire hook and hang them on a bar of the oven shelf with a drip tray underneath.
Bake for 30 minutes in the oven preheated to 475°F. or Gas Mark 9.
Very thinly slice the meat across the grain. Place the pieces in a heated serving dish and pour the juices from the drip tray over them.
Garnish with parsley.

NGOW YUK YUNG CHUNG
RUMP STEAK WITH ONION

Preparation time   3-4 minutes
Cooking time   7-8 minutes
To serve   3

You will need

4 oz. rump steak
1 Spanish onion
2 tablespoons peanut oil
1 crushed clove garlic
¼ pint (U.S. ⅝ cup) hot chicken stock
½ teaspoon ginger sherry (see page 151)
pinch each salt, sugar and Ve-Tsin
    (see page 151)
¼ teaspoon soy sauce
¾ teaspoon cornflour
1 dessertspoon cold water

Cut the rump steak into slices on the bias and then
into very thin strips across the grain.
Halve the onion and cut it into very thin slices.
Pour 1 tablespoon oil into the frying-pan and cook
the onion in it until browned. Remove it.
Wipe out the pan. Put in the remaining oil and let
it get very hot. Fry the garlic till golden and then
discard it.
In the same oil, fry the meat for 1 minute, remove it
and add it to the onion.
Add to the pan the stock, ginger sherry, seasonings
and soy sauce. Bring to the boil then stir in the
cornflour, blended with the water. Boil for 1½ minutes. Return the beef and onion to the pan and
heat through for ½ minute.

Turn the mixture into a heated dish and serve.

CHOW MIN YONG
FILLET OF LAMB
WITH VEGETABLES

Preparation time   15 minutes
Cooking time   5-6 minutes
To serve   2-3

You will need

4 oz. lamb (no fat)
½ teaspoon cornflour
½ beaten egg to bind
salt and pepper
2 tablespoons peanut oil
1 green pepper, cut in pieces
1 tablespoon Chinese mushrooms soaked 1 hour
    (see page 150), cut in very fine strips
1 tablespoon celery, cut in very fine strips
1 tablespoon spring onions
1 dessertspoon dry white wine
tiny pinch Ve-Tsin (see page 151)
½ tablespoon soy sauce
1 clove garlic, finely chopped
pinch white pepper

Cut the lamb in extremely thin strips. Work in the
cornflour and the egg thoroughly with a little salt
and pepper. Heat very well the peanut oil in a frying-
pan and fry the meat in it for 1 minute stirring it
and tossing it all the time. Add the green pepper,
Chinese mushrooms and celery and toss and cook

for 1 minute. Turn on to a sieve to drain the oil off. To the frying-pan add the onions and toss about. Return the meat and vegetables to the frying-pan. Add dry white wine, Ve-Tsin, soy sauce, finely chopped clove garlic and white pepper. Heat through and toss about and turn on to a hot dish and serve.

YUK PIN CHOW YER CHOY
PORK WITH CABBAGE

Preparation time   5-6 minutes
Cooking time   9-10 minutes
To serve   3

You will need

1 small cone-shaped cabbage heart
pinch each salt and Ve-Tsin (see page 151)
sugar
tiny pinch pepper
1½ teaspoons cornflour
5 teaspoons water
4 oz. pork, cut in thin strips
2 tablespoons peanut oil
1 crushed clove garlic
½ teaspoon ginger sherry (see page 151)
¼ pint (U.S. ⅝ cup) hot chicken stock
¼ teaspoon soy sauce

Separate the cabbage leaves and then break them

Pork with cabbage

up roughly but in not too small pieces. Drop them into boiling water. Boil them for 4 minutes, then drain them very well. Blend together the salt, Ve-Tsin, pepper, pinch of sugar and 1 teaspoon cornflour and 1 teaspoon water and work them well into the meat.

Get 1 tablespoon oil very hot in the frying-pan. Cook the cabbage pieces in it for 1 minute, while moving them about. Remove them.

Wipe out the pan. Heat the remaining oil in it. Fry the garlic to a pale gold colour and then discard it. Quickly fry the pork in the oil for 4 minutes. Add another pinch of sugar, sherry, chicken stock and soy sauce. Bring to the boil. Stir in the remaining cornflour, blended with the rest of the water and boil for 1½ minutes.

Return the cabbage to the pan and heat through.

CHAR SHIU
BARBECUED PORK

(Illustrated in colour on page 113)

Preparation time   15-20 minutes
Cooking time   40 minutes
To serve   3-4

You will need

2 strips raw leg of pork
ginger powder
finely chopped garlic
1 dessertspoon soya bean (see page 151)
1 dessertspoon red bean curd
¼-½ teaspoon ginger sherry (see page 151)
good pinch each salt and Ve-Tsin
   (see page 151)
very generous pinch sugar
sprinkling Chinese red colouring powder
cucumber, lettuce and parsley

Have the pork cut into two 6-inch strips, 1½ inches thick and 1½ inches wide. Dust them with the ginger powder and garlic. In a basin, mix together the soya bean, bean curd, sherry, salt, Ve-Tsin and sugar. Mash them until they are completely mixed. Lay the pieces of pork in an oiled baking tin. Work the above mixture and then the colouring powder into them on both sides. Place the tin in the hottest part of the oven, preheated to 400°F. or Gas Mark 6, and bake for 25 minutes. Turn and bake for a further 15 minutes.

Leave to become cold. Cut into slices and garnish with cucumber, lettuce and parsley.

CHENG DOW YUK DING

LEG OF PORK WITH CASHEW NUTS

Preparation time   5-6 minutes
Cooking time   6-8 minutes
To serve   2-3

You will need

3 tablespoons very thin slices lean raw pork
1 teaspoon cornflour
1 teaspoon ginger sherry (see page 151)
salt and Ve-Tsin (see page 151)
pepper
1 tablespoon raw carrot
1 tablespoon canned bamboo shoots
1 tablespoon canned water chestnuts
2-3 shoots fresh sprouting broccoli
1 medium-sized onion
peanut oil
5-6 tablespoons hot chicken stock
few drops sesame oil
$\frac{1}{4}$ teaspoon soy sauce
1 small teaspoon cornflour
1 dessertspoon water
2-3 tablespoons roasted cashew nuts

Place the pork slices in a basin. Add the cornflour, ginger sherry, pinch salt, Ve-Tsin and a few shakes pepper and work them well into the meat. Leave while preparing the vegetables.

Cut the carrot into match sticks. Slice the bamboo shoots and chestnuts and cut the broccoli into suitable pieces.

Keep the vegetables separate. Roughly chop the onion.

Put enough oil to deep fry to heat slowly. Meanwhile, heat 1 tablespoon oil in a frying-pan and fry the onion in it for $1\frac{1}{2}$-2 minutes, tossing it about. Add the carrot and toss for $\frac{1}{2}$ minute, then add the bamboo shoots, chestnuts and broccoli and cook for a further $\frac{1}{2}$ minute. Add the stock, another pinch salt, Ve-Tsin, few shakes pepper, the remaining ginger sherry, sesame oil and soy sauce and boil for 2 minutes, moving the vegetables about to cook them evenly.

If the deep oil, by this time, has reached a temperature of 375°F. or 190°C. — that is when a dried slice of raw potato rises fairly quickly from the bottom when dropped into it — add the pork. Blend the cornflour with the water and stir the vegetables into them. Boil for $1\frac{1}{2}$ minutes.

Turn the mixture into a heated serving dish and keep hot.

Wipe out the frying-pan. Add 1 teaspoon of peanut oil to it. When it is really hot, add the cashew nuts and turn them about in the oil to heat through for $\frac{1}{4}$ minutes. Mix them into the vegetables. The pork, by this time, will be a golden brown. Drain the pieces very well, place them on top of the vegetables and serve at once.

CHON TIEN KAI TOI

FROGS' LEGS

Preparation time   8-10 minutes
Cooking time   5 minutes
To serve   2

You will need

3 teaspoons dry white wine
10 frog's legs
3 tablespoons peanut oil
1 Chinese mushroom soaked 1 hour, thinly diced
1 tablespoon green sweet pepper, diced
1 tablespoon canned bamboo shoots, diced
1 tablespoon spring onion, cut in strips
1 clove garlic finely chopped
1 small teaspoon fresh ginger, finely chopped
1 tablespoon chicken stock
good pinch Ve-Tsin (see page 151)
tiny pinch salt
1 teaspoon cornflour

Work 1 teaspoon wine into the frogs's legs and then the cornflour and leave aside. Have ready the remaining ingredients and arrange in little heaps on a longish plate.

Heat till very hot the peanut oil in the frying-pan. Add the frog's legs, toss and shake over high heat for 2-3 minutes, then add the mushroom, sweet green pepper and bamboo shoots tossing and shaking them. Drain on a sieve.

Add the onion, garlic and ginger to the pan without adding any more oil.

Then the chicken stock, Ve-Tsin, the salt, the rest of the dry white wine and cook for $\frac{1}{2}$ minute. Return the frog's legs and vegetables to the pan. Heat through $\frac{1}{2}$ minute and serve.

Sweet-sour pork

Roast belly of pork

GEE YUK YER CHOY

BELLY PORK
WITH WHITE CABBAGE

Preparation time 7-8 minutes
Cooking time 6-7 minutes
To serve 2-3

You will need

3 tablespoons belly pork
salt and Ve-Tsin (see page 151)
few shakes white pepper
½ teaspoon ginger sherry*
few drops sesame oil
1 teaspoon cornflour
3 teaspoons water
4-5 tablespoons white cabbage
5 teaspoons peanut oil
1 clove garlic
2 thin slices fresh ginger
1 teaspoon black soya bean
4-5 tablespoons hot chicken stock
½ teaspoon sugar
2 spring onions

* Cut 2 oz. fresh ginger into thin strips. Turn the strips into a bottle and cover with half a bottle warm brown sherry. Leave to infuse, strain and use as directed.

After removing the rind, cut the pork into strips ⅛-inch wide. Place them in a basin with a pinch salt, pinch Ve-Tsin, few shakes pepper, ginger sherry, sesame oil, ½ teaspoon cornflour and 1 teaspoon water and work them well into the meat. Cut the cabbage into ¼-inch strips. (If white cabbage is not available, the inner leaves of pale green cabbage will do very well.) Drop the strips into slightly salted boiling water with 1 teaspoon oil in it. Boil for 5 minutes, drain, rinse in cold water and drain again.
Mash the crushed clove of garlic, ginger and black bean to a paste.
Heat the remaining oil in a frying-pan and fry the paste in it for ½ minute. Add the pork and cook it for 4 minutes. Next, add another pinch salt, pinch Ve-Tsin, few shakes pepper, stock, sugar and onions, (cut into 1¼-inch pieces). Finally, blend ½ teaspoon cornflour with the remaining water, stir it in and boil for 1½ minutes.
Turn into a heated dish and serve.

NG HEUNG NGOW
YUK NGAR CHOY

'FIVE-PERFUMED' BEEF
WITH BEAN SPROUTS

Preparation time 5-6 minutes
Cooking time 6-8 minutes
To serve 2-3

You will need

1 small piece dried tangerine
   rind (½-inch in size)
2-3 slices fresh ginger
tiniest possible pinch cumin powder
3 tablespoons rump steak
½ teaspoon ginger sherry (see previous recipe)
few drops sesame oil
salt, sugar and Ve-Tsin (see page 151)
pepper
1 scant teaspoon cornflour
1 teaspoon water
2 tablespoons peanut oil
2-3 tablespoons chicken stock*
good handful bean sprouts (see page 102)

* If no chicken stock is available use a chicken bouillon cube with water.

In advance, soak the tangerine rind in water, with the chill removed, to soften it a little. Cut the rind and the ginger into thin strips. Add the cumin powder.
Cut the steak into match sticks.
Place the sticks of steak in a basin with the ginger sherry, sesame oil, pinch each salt, sugar, Ve-Tsin, few shakes pepper, cornflour and water and work all together. Heat until very hot 1 tablespoon of the peanut oil in a frying-pan.
Cook the steak in it for 2 minutes, tossing and turning it about, then remove the meat.
Turn the tangerine mixture into the same pan with the chicken stock and cook for 2 minutes. Meanwhile, heat the remaining oil in another pan. Add the bean sprouts (picked over and with any empty seed cases discarded) and an extra pinch salt and Ve-Tsin and cook for 2 minutes. Combine the meat with the tangerine mixture, add to the bean sprouts and heat through. Turn all into a heated dish and serve.

GU LO YUK
SWEET-SOUR PORK

(Illustrated in colour on page 85)
Preparation time   25-30 minutes
Cooking time   25-30 minutes
To serve   3-4

You will need

4-6 oz. 1-inch cubes lean leg pork
pinch each pepper, salt and Ve-Tsin
  (see page 151)
½ teaspoon sesame oil
½ teaspoon ginger sherry (see page 151)
1 tablespoon self-raising flour
peanut oil for deep frying

BATTER

3 oz. self-raising flour
½ small egg
¼ pint (U.S. ⅝ cup) water
½ teaspoon peanut oil

SWEET-SOUR SAUCE

1 dessertspoon sugar
tiny pinch each pepper, salt and Ve-Tsin
1½-2 tablespoons malt vinegar
½ teaspoon soy sauce
¾ teaspoon tomato ketchup
13 dessertspoons water
¾ teaspoon cornflour

VEGETABLE GARNISH

1 tablespoon each pickled cabbage, carrot
  and cucumber
salt
vinegar

TO MAKE THE BATTER

Sift the flour into a basin. Make a well in the centre, drop in the egg then gradually add and beat in the water. Finally, stir in the oil. Set aside for 20 minutes.

TO MAKE THE SWEET-SOUR SAUCE

Bring the first 7 ingredients and 12 dessertspoons water to the boil. Stir in the cornflour, blended with the remaining water, and cook for 1½ minutes. Keep hot.

TO MAKE VEGETABLE GARNISH

Cut the vegetables julienne style — that is, into thin strips. Sprinkle with ⅓ teaspoon salt and leave for 5-6 minutes. Press out the liquid. Sprinkle with a little more salt and just enough vinegar to flavour them.

TO PREPARE THE PORK

Place the pork in a basin. Add the seasonings, sesame oil, and sherry and work them well into the meat.
Coat the diced pork with the flour. Turn the cubes into a sieve and toss about to shake off excess flour. Drop the meat into the batter.
As the pork has to be cooked through, have the oil heated to 360°F. or 182°C. Drop the pork into it and cook for 8-9 minutes.
Raise the heat and cook the pork to a warm golden tone.
Drain and dry on absorbent paper.
Turn the pork into a heated serving dish, deep enough to contain all the ingredients. Add the pickled vegetables and spoon the sweet-sour sauce over them.

NGOW YUK SAN CHOY
RUMP STEAK AND COS LETTUCE

Preparation time   5-6 minutes
Cooking time   5-6 minutes
To serve   3

You will need

4 oz. rump steak
2 thin slices fresh ginger (see page 151)
salt, sugar and Ve-Tsin (see page 151)
1 teaspoon cornflour
3 teaspoons water
½ teaspoon soy sauce
1 small cos lettuce
2 tablespoons peanut oil
1 crushed clove garlic
½ teaspoon ginger sherry (see page 151)
¼ pint (U.S. ⅝ cup) hot chicken stock

Cut the steak and ginger into thin strips. Place them in a basin. Add a pinch salt, sugar and Ve-Tsin, ½ teaspoon cornflour, 1 teaspoon water and ¼ teaspoon soy sauce; work them well into the meat and set aside. Cut the lettuce across in 2-inch pieces.
Pour 1 tablespoon oil into the frying-pan and make it very hot. Fry the lettuce in it for 1 minute, moving it about to coat it with the oil. Lift it out.
Wipe out the pan. Add the remaining oil and make it very hot. Fry the garlic till pale gold and then discard it. Add the steak, ginger and ginger sherry and fry quickly for 1-2 minutes. Remove.
Add the stock, another pinch salt, sugar and Ve-Tsin and the remaining soy sauce and the rest of the

cornflour, blended with the remaining water and boil for 1½ minutes.

Finally, add the meat, ginger and lettuce and cook for a further minute.

Turn all into a heated dish and serve.

CHOW NGOW CHI YEW FAR
VEAL KIDNEY, YUNNAN STYLE

Preparation time   8-10 minutes
Cooking time   5-6 minutes
To serve   2-3

You will need

3-4 tablespoons sliced veal kidney*

2 tablespoons green sweet pepper

1 tablespoon Chinese mushrooms (see page 150)

1 tablespoon water chestnuts

2 tablespoons peanut oil

salt and Ve-Tsin (see page 151)

pepper

¼-½ teaspoon soy sauce

½ teaspoon ginger sherry (see page 151)

3-4 tablespoons hot chicken stock

½ teaspoon cornflour

1 dessertspoon water

1 crushed clove garlic

* The slices of kidney should be about ⅛-inch thick and the core and tissue bits running from it into the flesh should be discarded.

Set the kidney slices aside.

Thinly slice the pepper, mushrooms and chestnuts.

Have the vegetables ready.

Heat 1 tablespoon of the oil in a frying-pan. Quickly fry the pepper in it for 1 minute. Add the mushrooms and cook them 1 minute, then the chestnuts and cook for further ½ minute. Add a pinch of salt, a pinch Ve-Tsin, a few shakes of pepper, soy sauce, sherry and stock and bring to the boil.

Stir in the cornflour, blended with the water, and boil for 1½ minutes.

Meanwhile, heat the remaining oil in another pan, fry the garlic in it till a pale gold colour and then discard it.

Sprinkle a little pepper, salt and Ve-Tsin into the kidneys and quickly fry them for 1 minute at high heat.

Turn the vegetable mixture into a heated serving dish and place the kidney on top.

Note

In this instance, the kidney is fried *after* the vegetable garnish has been cooked. This is because kidney is at its best only when cooked and served at once. It cannot wait for even a quarter of a minute without becoming hard and losing half its charm.

This remark also applies to all meat cooked the Chinese way.

I would, therefore, urge enthusiasts for Chinese food to use two pans, whenever possible, when meat is part of a dish.

The Chinese cook may manage with one but, when it comes to speedy cooking, he is probably the most expert chef in the world.

NGOW YUK HAM CHOY
BEEF WITH PRESERVED MUSTARD PLANT

Preparation time   4-5 minutes
Cooking time   4-5 minutes
To serve   2-3

You will need

salt and Ve-Tsin (see page 151)
ginger sherry*
1½ teaspoons cornflour
2-3 tablespoons rump steak, cut diagonally into thin slices
3 tablespoons preserved Chinese mustard plant (see page 150)
2-3 thin slices fresh ginger
1 clove garlic
1 tablespoon black soya bean
peanut oil
4-5 tablespoons hot chicken stock
few drops sesame oil
½ teaspoon soy sauce
1 tablespoon water

* Cut 2 oz. fresh ginger into thin strips. Turn the strips into a bottle and cover with half a bottle warm brown sherry. Leave to infuse, strain and use as directed.

Work a tiny pinch salt, Ve-Tsin, few drops ginger sherry and ½ teaspoon cornflour into the meat slices and place ready.
Have the mustard plant ready, too.
Crush the ginger, garlic and black bean and mix together to a smooth paste.
Have enough oil for deep frying gradually heating. Heat 1 tablespoon of oil in a frying-pan, add the ginger-garlic-bean paste and cook for ½ minute, stirring. Add the stock, another pinch salt and pinch Ve-Tsin, ½ teaspoon ginger sherry, sesame oil and soy sauce and heat through. Add the mustard plant and cook for 2-3 minutes. The deep oil, by this time, should have reached a temperature of 375°F. or 190°C. — that is, when a dried slice of raw potato rises to the surface in a few seconds when dropped into it.
Add the meat and cook for 3 minutes.
Blend 1 teaspoon cornflour with the water, stir it into the vegetable mixture and cook for 1½ minutes.
Add the drained meat.
At once turn the mixture into a heated serving dish.

Pork and cauliflower

YUK PIN CHOW CHOY FAR
PORK AND CAULIFLOWER

Preparation time   8-9 minutes
Cooking time   6-8 minutes
To serve   3

You will need

4 oz. lean leg pork
6 cauliflower fleurets
salt
pinch pepper
½ teaspoon soy sauce
5 teaspoons pork dripping
1 teaspoon cornflour
2 dessertspoons water
2 crushed cloves garlic
pinch sugar and Ve-Tsin (see page 151)
4 tablespoons chicken stock

Cut the pork on the bias and then into thin slices. Set aside. Parboil the cauliflower fleurets for 5-6 minutes. Drain them well. Add a pinch of salt, pepper, the soy sauce and 1 teaspoon of melted pork dripping. Blend ½ teaspoon cornflour in 1 desertspoon water and toss the fleurets in it. Quickly fry them in 2 dessertspoons of the dripping. Transfer them to a heated dish. Wipe out the pan. Melt the remaining dripping in it. Quickly fry the pork. Add a pinch of salt, sugar and Ve-Tsin, the chicken stock and the remaining cornflour blended in the rest of the water. Return the fleurets to the pan and heat through. Turn all into a heated dish and serve.

Rump steak and soya bean curd

Rump steak in oyster sauce

SEE JOP NGOW YUK
RUMP STEAK AND SOYA BEAN CURD

Preparation time　2-3 minutes
Cooking time　6 minutes
To serve　3

You will need

4 oz. rump steak
salt, sugar and Ve-Tsin
　(see page 151)
1 tablespoon yellow soya beans (beans crushed)
1 tablespoon peanut oil
1 crushed clove garlic
$\frac{1}{4}$ pint (U.S. $\frac{5}{8}$ cup) hot chicken stock
$\frac{1}{4}$ teaspoon soy sauce
$\frac{1}{2}$ teaspoon cornflour
1 dessertspoon cold water

Cut steak into thin slices across the grain. Put in a basin and thoroughly work in a pinch salt, sugar and Ve-Tsin and crushed soya beans. Heat about three-quarters of the oil in frying-pan.
Cook garlic in it until pale gold; discard it.
Add meat and cook it at a high heat for 1-2 minutes, tossing and turning it in the pan.
Lift meat out.
Add the remaining oil and the chicken stock, sauce and another pinch salt, sugar and Ve-Tsin to the pan and bring them to the boil.
Blend the cornflour with the water; stir it in and boil for $1\frac{1}{2}$ minutes.
Return the meat to the pan and boil up once.
Turn all into a heated dish and serve.

HOYOW NGOW YUK
RUMP STEAK IN OYSTER SAUCE

Preparation time　4-5 minutes
Cooking time　4-5 minutes
To serve　2-3

You will need

4 oz. rump steak, cut in thin slices
2 thin slices fresh ginger (see page 151)
salt, sugar and Ve-Tsin (see page 151)
$\frac{1}{4}$ teaspoon soy sauce
1 teaspoon cornflour
3 teaspoons cold water
1 tablespoon peanut oil
2 crushed cloves garlic
$\frac{1}{2}$ teaspoon ginger sherry (see page 151)
$\frac{1}{4}$ pint (U.S. $\frac{5}{8}$ cup) hot chicken stock
1 dessertspoon oyster sauce
parsley

Place steak and ginger in a basin. Add a pinch salt, sugar and Ve-Tsin, $\frac{1}{2}$ teaspoon cornflour and 1 teaspoon water and work them well into the meat. Heat the oil. Fry the garlic in it until golden and then discard it. Fry the meat in the oil for 1-2 minutes; then remove. To the pan add the sherry, stock and another pinch salt, sugar and Ve-Tsin and bring to the boil. Add the oyster sauce and the remaining cornflour, blended with the rest of the water, and boil for $1\frac{1}{2}$ minutes. Return the meat to the pan and heat through for $\frac{1}{2}$ minute.
Turn all into a heated serving dish and garnish with parsley.

FOO GWAR NGOW YUK
BEEF WITH BITTER MELON

Preparation time   7-8 minutes
Cooking time   7-8 minutes
To serve   2-3

You will need

2-3 tablespoons raw rump steak
salt and Ve-Tsin (see page 151)
ginger sherry (see page 151)
½ teaspoon cornflour
3 tablespoons bitter melon (see page 150)
2-3 thin slices fresh ginger
1 clove garlic
1 tablespoon black soya beans (see page 151)
peanut oil
few drops sesame oil
½ teaspoon soy sauce
1 dessertspoon sugar
4-5 tablespoons hot chicken stock
1 level teaspoon cornflour
1 tablespoon water

Cut the steak diagonally into thin slices.
Add a tiny pinch salt, tiny pinch Ve-Tsin, few drops sherry, ½ teaspoon cornflour and work well into the steak.
Cut the bitter melon into strips and drop them into boiling water for 5 minutes.
Drain, drop into cold water to crisp them and drain again.
Crush the ginger, garlic and black bean and mix them together to a paste.
Let enough oil for deep frying be heating gradually. Heat 1 tablespoon of oil in a frying-pan.
Add the ginger-garlic-bean mixture and the bitter melon and cook for a few seconds, tossing and moving them about.
Add ½ teaspoon ginger sherry, sesame oil, soy sauce, sugar (because the melon is still a little bitter), stock and another pinch salt and pinch Ve-Tsin.
Bring to the boil and cook for 3 minutes.
The deep oil should by now have reached a temperature of 375°F. or 190°C. — that is when a dried slice of raw potato, dropped into it, rises quickly to the surface.
Fry the steak in it for 2-3 minutes.
Blend the cornflour with the water, stir it into the first mixture and boil for 1½ minutes. Add the drained fried meat.
Turn all into a heated dish and serve.

Rump steak and celery

NGOW YUK KAN CHOY
RUMP STEAK AND CELERY

Preparation time   7-8 minutes
Cooking time   6-7 minutes
To serve   3-4

You will need

4 oz. rump steak
3 thin slices fresh ginger (see page 151)
2-3 inside sticks crisp celery
9 teaspoons peanut oil
salt, sugar and Ve-Tsin (see page 151)
hot chicken stock
cornflour
2 dessertspoons water
1 crushed clove garlic
½ teaspoon soy sauce

Cut meat into thin slices and ginger into thin strips. Halve celery lengthwise; cut it slantwise in 2-3-inch lengths. Place meat and ginger in a basin. Add 1 teaspoon oil, tiny pinch salt, sugar and Ve-Tsin, 1 tablespoon stock and pinch cornflour, blended with 1 dessertspoon water. Work them into the meat. Heat 4 teaspoons oil and fry celery in it for 1 minute, tossing and turning it. Remove celery. Wipe out pan, heat remaining oil in it. Fry garlic till golden and discard it. Add meat and ginger to pan. Fry for 3 minutes, tossing them about. Remove them. Add ¼ pint (U. S. ⅝ cup) stock, pinch salt, sugar and Ve-Tsin and soy sauce. Bring to the boil. Stir in 1 level teaspoon cornflour, blended with 1 dessertspoon water, and cook for 1½ minutes. Return beef and celery to pan; heat.

Pork meat balls

YUK SEE NGAR CHOY
PORK AND BEAN SPROUTS

Preparation time   10 minutes
Cooking time   7-10 minutes
To serve   2-3

You will need

3 large tablespoons shredded raw pork
1 teaspoon peanut oil
pinch salt
pinch sugar
pinch Ve-Tsin (see page 151)
1 teaspoon soy sauce
1 teaspoon ginger sherry (see page 151)
2 cloves garlic
8 oz. bean sprouts
pork dripping
4-5 tablespoons stock
1 teaspoon cornflour
1 tablespoon water
1 onion 'flower' (see page 49)

Cut the pork into thinnish strips and place them in a bowl.
Add the next 6 ingredients and 1 finely chopped clove of garlic and work them very well into the meat. Set aside.
Pick over the sprouts to get rid of any seeds.
Melt 1 tablespoon dripping and cook the bean sprouts in it for under 2 minutes. Remove the sprouts. Add a little more pork dripping and then crush the other clove of garlic, adding it to the bean sprouts. After ¼ minute, discard the garlic. Raise the heat. Add the pork and move it about for

2-3 minutes.
Add the stock, bring to the boil then add the cornflour, blended with the water. Add the bean sprouts and heat through, tossing all about.
Turn into a heated serving dish and garnish with the onion 'flower'.

CHAR YUK YIN
PORK MEAT BALLS

Preparation time   20 minutes
Cooking time   10 minutes
To serve   2-3

You will need

6 oz. pork (about ¼ of it fat)
1 dessertspoon canned water chestnuts
1 dessertspoon canned bamboo shoots
pinch each salt, sugar and Ve-Tsin
  (see page 151)
1 teaspoon beaten egg
1 tablespoon self-raising flour
peanut oil
parsley sprigs

BATTER

2 tablespoons self-raising flour
scant ¼ pint (U.S. ½ cup) water

Finely chop the pork, water chestnuts and bamboo shoots.
Add the seasonings and the beaten egg.
Having worked the mixture well together, throw it down on the table as you would when making dough in order to get everything well combined.
Divide into 5—6 pieces and roll each into a neat ball between the palms of the hands.
Turn the balls in the flour and then in a thin batter made with the flour and the water.
Leave to rest for a few minutes. Get the oil fairly hot.
As the meat is raw and has to be cooked through, the oil should not be so hot that it browns the surface of the balls too quickly.
Dip a spoon in the oil and then use it to transfer each ball to the oil. After 8 minutes, raise the heat to brown the balls. Lift out and drain the balls.
Place them in a heated serving dish and garnish them with sprigs of parsley.

SUB GUM NGOW YUK
FILLET STEAK WITH MIXED VEGETABLES

(Illustrated in colour on page 95)
Preparation time   7-8 minutes
Cooking time   6-8 minutes
To serve   3-4

You will need

3 oz. fillet steak, very thinly cut across
    the grain
sugar
tiny pinch pepper
few drops ginger sherry (see page 151)
few drops sesame oil
½ egg white
½ teaspoon cornflour
1 teaspoon water
2½ tablespoons peanut oil
several thin slices cucumber
3-4 strips celery
3-4 strips green sweet pepper
3-4 strips red sweet pepper
tiny pinch each salt and Ve-Tsin (see page 151)
¼ teaspoon soy sauce
½ teaspoon sesame oil
1 finely chopped small clove garlic
1 teaspoon vinegar
boiled rice, Chinese style (see page 128)

Place meat in a basin. Add pinch sugar, tiny pinch
pepper, sherry, sesame oil, egg white, cornflour and
water.
Work well together with fingers; lift out mixture;
throw back into basin. Repeat to force dressing
into meat. Leave aside. Heat ½ tablespoon oil in
frying pan. Add vegetables, except for garlic, salt,
pinch sugar and Ve-Tsin, soy sauce and sesame oil.
Toss all about for 3-4 minutes. Put on heated
dish; keep hot. Wipe out pan. Heat remaining oil.
Add garlic, meat mixture and vinegar and quickly
cook for 1 minute over high heat. Turn mixture on
to vegetables. Serve boiled rice separately.

BOR LOW GU LO YUK
SWEET SOUR PORK WITH PINEAPPLE

Preparation time   6-8 minutes
Cooking time   8-10 minutes
To serve   2-3

You will need

3 oz. cooked lean raw pork *
peanut oil
1 tablespoon green sweet pepper, diced
1 small onion, chopped
1 teaspoon tomato purée
2 small tablespoons sugar
pinch salt
2 tablespoons chicken stock
2 tablespoons wine vinegar
1 small teaspoon cornflour
1 dessertspoon water
2 tablespoons ripe tomato wedges
2 tablespoons canned pineapple wedges,
    chopped
¼ small chopped chilli, pounded to paste

* The pork should be cooked to a pale cream colour
and left to become cold.

Cut pork into ¾-inch dice; fry in deep peanut oil
hot enough to give it a pale golden colour in 3 minutes.
Drain and leave to become cold.
Cut pepper into strips and place ready. Heat
1 tablespoon peanut oil in frying-pan. Fry onion,
tossing it about so that it cooks but does not colour.
Remove from heat and work in tomato purée and
sugar, add salt and chicken stock and return to
heat. Add vinegar. Meanwhile turn pork into very
hot oil to brown. Blend cornflour and water and
stir into sauce in frying-pan. Add green pepper
and cook for 1 minute, add tomatoes, and cook
½ minute, add pineapple and chilli; toss for about
½ minute. Meanwhile when pork is a rich gold,
drain thoroughly and turn into frying-pan with
other ingredients. Toss them together for a moment.
Put on a dish and serve.

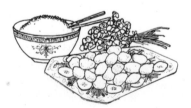

Fillet steak with mixed vegetables; boiled rice

Chinese salad

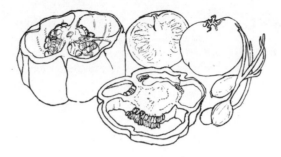

VEGETABLES

CHOY

If the Chinese had contributed to our Western kitchen nothing further than their way of cooking and presenting vegetables, they would still have done us a great service.

Here, as in all their cooking, speed is the essential. Watercress in this country is used, for the most part, as a garnish or an addition to salads. One has only to cook it the Chinese way to realise what a tasty 'green' it is.

We are told to cook the outer leaves of lettuce but the long process given to them by Western cooks does nothing for them. The Chinese way gives us almost a new vegetable — certainly lettuce with an infinitely better taste.

And so it is with green beans and green sweet peppers. They need only the quick Chinese method to be cooked to perfection. Other vegetables such as broccoli, cauliflower and carrots may be blanched (parboiled) then finished off in a little oil in the frying-pan.

Bean sprouts are typically Chinese and, as such, are 'exotic' to us. The beans are very easy to 'sprout', provided the directions are followed carefully (see page 102).

CHUNG KOK SANG
CHINESE SALAD

(Illustrated in colour on opposite page)

Preparation time   few minutes
Cooking time   few minutes
To serve   2

You will need

2 tablespoons bean sprouts
2 tablespoons shredded pickled carrots
   (in jars)
2 tablespoons shredded pickled cabbage
   (in jars)
1 tablespoon shredded green pepper
2 rings canned pineapple
1 good-sized firm ripe tomato or 2 small
   ones
1 lettuce heart

Pick over the beans sprouts then drop them into boiling water for 3-4 minutes. Drain, pour cold water over them and drain very well again.

Combine the sprouts with the well drained pickled vegetables and the green pepper. Place them on a serving dish and garnish with the pineapple rings (each halved, slantwise), halved large tomato or whole small ones and halved heart of lettuce.

HOME-MADE PICKLES

If you wish to pickle the vegetables at home, this is the way to go about it: wash and drain the carrots and cabbage. Cut them into suitable strips and leave them for most of the day.

Bring ¾ pint (U.S. scant 2 cups) water to the boil. Add ½ teaspoon salt, 1 slice fresh ginger, 2 chillis, 3 crushed peppercorns, 1 teaspoon ginger sherry (see page 151) and a good pinch of Ve-Tsin (see page 151). Leave to become cold. Turn the shredded vegetables into a suitable jar and pour the mixture over them. Cover and leave for 1-2 days in warm weather or up to 5 days in the winter. Turn the vegetables into a colander and leave to drain thoroughly.

SUB GUM CHOY SEE

JULIENNE OF VEGETABLES

Preparation time 5-6 minutes
Cooking time 5 minutes
To serve 2-3

You will need

2 oz. carrots
2 oz. white cabbage
2 oz. green pepper
2 oz. celery
1 tablespoon peanut oil
1 crushed clove garlic
1 slice fresh ginger *
$\frac{1}{4}$ pint (U.S. $\frac{5}{8}$ cup) chicken stock
small pinch each salt, sugar and Ve-Tsin
  (see page 151)
dash pepper
$\frac{1}{2}$ teaspoon soy sauce
1 teaspoon cornflour
1 tablespoon cold water

* This is different from dried root ginger as it is moist and almost juicy. It is cut into slices or shreds.

Cut the vegetables into very thin 2-3-inch strips. Heat the oil in a frying-pan. Add the garlic. When golden discard it. Add the ginger and almost immediately the stock and vegetables. Cook for 2 minutes, moving them about.

Add the seasonings and soy sauce and cook them for $\frac{1}{4}$ minute. Blend the cornflour with the water and stir it into the boiling mixture. Gently cook for $1\frac{1}{2}$ minutes. Turn into a heated dish and serve.

Note

This julienne of vegetables is also used as a garnish for Chinese dishes. Especially useful if you want to make a dish look bigger than it is.

WUI TUNG GOO

FRIED CHINESE MUSHROOMS

Preparation time overnight soaking
Cooking time about 25 minutes
To serve 2-3

You will need

3-4 Chinese mushrooms (see page 150)
1 tablespoon peanut oil
5 slices fresh root ginger (see page 151)
$\frac{1}{2}$ pint (U.S. $1\frac{1}{4}$ cups) chicken stock
pinch each salt, sugar and Ve-Tsin
  (see page 151)
3 drops soy sauce
1 teaspoon cornflour
1 tablespoon cold water
1 onion 'flower' (see page 49)

When Chinese mushrooms are used in a dish, they

Julienne of vegetables

98

Fried Chinese mushrooms

require preliminary preparation. After removing the stalks, soak the mushrooms in cold water overnight.
Next day wash and drain them, then cover with chicken stock and cook them for 10 minutes. Drain and they are ready to be used as directed. In this case slice straight across the mushroom, giving four pieces. Heat the oil. Crush the ginger, fry it till golden and discard it. Add and fry the mushrooms for 2 minutes. Add the stock and boil hard for 10 minutes to reduce it. Add the seasonings during this time and the soy sauce. (This dish requires very little.)
Finally, blend the cornflour with the water, stir it in and continue to stir while boiling for 1½ minutes. Turn into a heated dish, decorate with an onion 'flower' and serve.

YOW SAN CHOY
QUICK STIR LETTUCE

Preparation time 1-2 minutes
Cooking time 1-2 minutes
To serve 2-3

You will need

1 Webb's wonder lettuce *
1 pint (U.S. 2½ cups) chicken or chicken cube stock
1 tablespoon peanut oil
½ teaspoon soy sauce
tiny pinch each salt and Ve-Tsin (see page 151)

* This is also known as 'iceberg lettuce'.

Remove enough of the hearty leaves of the lettuce to serve 2-3 persons.
Drop them into the boiling stock and cook for a bare minute.
Lift out and drain.
Get the oil and soy sauce very hot.
Drop the lettuce into them and heat through.
Add the seasonings. Turn the lettuce into a heated serving dish and pour the oil and soy sauce over them.

Quick stir lettuce

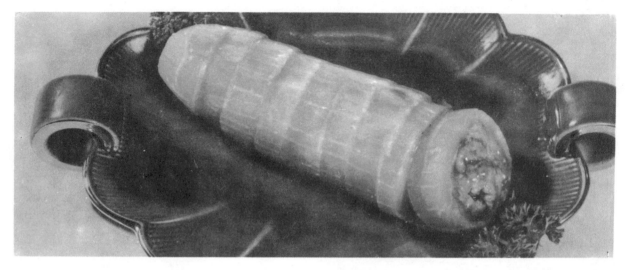

YEUNG CHENG KWAR
STUFFED CUCUMBER

Preparation time 10 minutes
Cooking time 20-25 minutes
To serve 3

You will need

½ good-sized cucumber
2½ oz. pork (a little fat with it)
1 generous teaspoon canned water chestnuts
1 generous teaspoon canned bamboo shoots
tiny pinch each salt, sugar and Ve-Tsin
   (see page 151)
½ teaspoon beaten egg
1 dessertspoon peanut oil
1 crushed clove garlic
4 tablespoons stock
¼ teaspoon soy sauce
½ teaspoon cornflour
1 dessertspoon cold water
parsley or watercress or onion 'flower'
   (see page 49)

Peel the cucumber. With a long thin pointed knife remove the seeds without cutting through the opposite end, leaving a fair-sized 'cave' in the cucumber. Very finely chop the pork, chestnuts and bamboo shoots. Mix them together and work in a tiny pinch of salt, sugar and Ve-Tsin and the beaten egg. Knead and throw as when making bread dough.
Stuff the cucumber with this filling and place it in a steamer, cover tightly and steam hard for 20 minutes.

Meanwhile, heat the oil. Fry the garlic in it until golden and then discard it. Add to the pan the stock, another pinch of salt, sugar and Ve-Tsin and the soy sauce. Bring to the boil. Stir in the cornflour, blended with the water, and boil for 1½-2 minutes.
Remove the cucumber to a heated serving dish. Cut it through into slices and spoon the sauce over them.
Garnish with parsley, watercress or onion 'flower'.

CHEN CHOW NGAR CHOY
BEAN SPROUTS
WITH SPRING ONIONS

Preparation time 3-4 minutes
Cooking time 2½-3 minutes
To serve 2-3

You will need

6-7 oz. bean sprouts
2-3 spring onions
1 crushed clove garlic
1 tablespoon peanut oil
4 tablespoons hot chicken stock
pinch each salt, sugar and Ve-Tsin
   (see page 151)

Pick over the bean sprouts, discarding any seeds.
Cut the onions into 1½-inch lengths.
Fry the garlic in the hot oil until golden and then discard it.

Add the bean sprouts and cook them for 2 minutes at high heat, stirring all the time.

Add and cook the onions for ¼ minutes. Add the stock and seasonings and boil together for ¼ minute. Turn into a heated dish and serve.

White heart of cabbage

YER CHOY

WHITE HEART OF CABBAGE

Preparation time   2-3 minutes
Cooking   12-13 minutes
To servtieme   2-3

You will need

1 heart of cabbage (about 4 oz.) *
1 dessertspoon peanut oil
1 slice fresh ginger (see page 151)
1 clove garlic
pinch each salt, sugar and Ve-Tsin (see page 151)
½ teaspoon soy sauce
4 tablespoons hot chicken stock
½ teaspoon cornflour
1 tablespoon cold water

* The heart of cabbage can be that of any one which is seasonal.
One would not, however, use hard white Dutch winter cabbage.

Cut the cabbage heart into 1- to 1½-inch pieces and separate each from the others. Drop them into ½ pint (U.S. 1¼ cups) boiling water and cook for 10 minutes. Drain thoroughly.

Heat the oil in a frying-pan. Crush the ginger and garlic and add to the oil and cook until the garlic is a deep golden colour. Discard it.

Add the cabbage and, in quick succession, the seasonings and soy sauce. Stir them about.

Add the chicken stock and cook for less than ½ minute. Blend the cornflour with the water and stir it in. Boil for 1½ minutes.

Turn all into a heated dish and serve.

Bean sprouts with spring onions

NGAR CHOY
BEAN SPROUTS

Some suppliers specialising in the raw materials required for Chinese cooking sell bean sprouts ready to use and, when you can get them, they do save time. In the Fu Tong restaurants, the beans are sprouted — that is, germinated — on the premises. I myself have 'sprouted' beans. Anyone who has grown mustard and cress on a wet cloth or blotting-paper will have no difficulty.

After the beans have germinated, the main thing to bear in mind is never to let the sprouts become fusty or mouldy.

The following method is a good one for success.

Buy a new large earthenware flower-pot. Scrub it well in plain water and then immerse it in clean cold water and leave it overnight.

Gently and quickly wash the beans by placing them in a colander under the cold tap and letting the water trickle through them. Drain them and transfer them to a basin. Cover with water warmed to 100°F. or 37°C. and leave overnight in a temperature of 70°-75°F. or 21°-23°C. (In the absence of a thermometer, judge the temperature of the water by remembering that blood heat is about 98°F. or 36°C.)

Next morning, drain the flower-pot. Stand it on two slats of wood with the hole between them. This is important to ensure the circulation of air. Drainage is also important. If the water does not drain away, the germinated beans could become musty and unfit for use. Place a piece of nylon (a nylon tea-strainer is ideal) over the hole.

Dry the beans and add them to the pot. Through them, pour water not warmer than 100°F. or 37°C. and cover with a damp cloth. Again leave them overnight in a temperature of 70°-75°F. or 21°-23°C.

Repeat the addition of water (not more than 100°F. or 37°C. in temperature) and the resting overnight at the above temperature on succeeding days and, in six days, the beans will have germinated to their full usable length and you will have sprouts a generous inch in length.

Fill the sink with cold water. Turn the sprouted beans into it and move them about in it so that the husks will float and can be removed. Drain and pick over, discarding any beans which have not germinated. If possible, use the sprouts the day they are ready. This also applies to any bean sprouts you have bought ready to use. You can buy beans sprouts in cans. But Mr. Fu Tong frowns on them — and so do I. In some cases, peas can be sprouted instead of beans, following the same method.

Mushrooms in white sauce

MOW GOO BAT JOP
MUSHROOMS IN WHITE SAUCE

Preparation time   3-4 minutes
Cooking time   6-8 minutes
To serve   3

You will need

6 white-capped unopened cultivated
   mushrooms *
1 tablespoon peanut oil
$\frac{1}{4}$ pint (U.S. $\frac{5}{8}$ cup) hot chicken stock
4 tablespoons cream of top milk
pinch each salt, sugar and Ve-Tsin
   (see page 151)
1 teaspoon cornflour
1 dessertspoon cold water
sprig parsley
* These should be $1\frac{1}{2}$-$1\frac{3}{4}$ inches in diameter.

Very quickly wash the unpeeled mushrooms in plain water. Dry them well.

Heat the oil. Cook the mushrooms on both sides in it for a minute or so, letting the caps become slightly browned. Add the hot stock and cook rapidly for 4 minutes.

By this time, the mushrooms may have absorbed the oil. In this case, add a little more. If the stock has evaporated too much, add up to another 4 tablespoons and bring to the boil again.

Add the top of milk, seasonings and cornflour, blended with the water, and boil for $1\frac{1}{2}$ minutes.

Lift the mushrooms on to a heated serving dish, spoon the sauce over them and garnish with the parsley.

GING AI KWAR
STEAMED AUBERGINE

Preparation time 6-8 minutes
Cooking time 20-25 minutes
To serve 2-3

You will need

1 fair-sized long type aubergine (eggplant)
3 oz. pork
1 tablespoon peanut oil
1 crushed clove garlic
pinch each salt, sugar and Ve-Tsin
  (see page 151)
$\frac{1}{4}$ teaspoon soy sauce
$\frac{1}{4}$ pint (U.S. $\frac{5}{8}$ cup) hot chicken stock
$\frac{1}{2}$ teaspoon cornflour
1 dessertspoon water
1 onion 'flower' (see page 49)

Wash the aubergine and steam it, tightly covered, for 20 minutes. Fairly finely chop the pork. Heat the oil. Fry the garlic till golden and discard it. Add and fry the pork for 2-3 minutes, during which time add the seasonings and soy sauce. Add the stock, bring to the boil, then add the cornflour, blended with the water. Boil for 1$\frac{1}{2}$ minutes.
Place the aubergine, cut on the bias, in a heated serving dish and spoon the pork and sauce over it. Garnish with the onion 'flower'.

CHOW MO GWAR
FRIED COURGETTE

Preparation time 2-3 minutes
Cooking time 6-7 minutes
To serve 2-3

You will need

1 6-7-inch courgette (zucchini or
  very young marrow)
1 crushed clove garlic
1 crushed thin slice fresh ginger
  (see page 151)
1 tablespoon peanut oil
pinch each salt, sugar and Ve-Tsin
  (see page 151)
2-3 shakes white pepper
$\frac{1}{2}$ teaspoon ginger sherry (see page 151)
$\frac{1}{4}$ pint (U.S. $\frac{5}{8}$ cup) hot chicken stock

If necessary peel the courgette thinly and then cut it diagonally into oval slices about $\frac{1}{4}$-inch thick. Fry the garlic and ginger in the oil until a golden colour and then discard them.
Add the slices of courgette and toss and turn them for 1 minute.
Sprinkle in the seasonings and sherry and turn over and over for $\frac{1}{2}$ minute.
Add the hot stock and cook for 4-5 minutes. Turn into a heated dish and serve.

Steamed aubergine

CHOW SUB GUM
FRIED MIXED VEGETABLES

Preparation time   8-10 minutes
Cooking time   8 minutes
To serve   3-4

You will need

2 Chinese mushrooms (see page 150)
1 small onion
½ green sweet pepper
3 oz. bean sprouts
5 canned water chestnuts
½ unpeeled cucumber
3 tablespoons celery
2 tablespoons peanut oil
6 slices canned bamboo shoots
¼ pint (U.S. ⅝ cup) hot stock
pinch each salt, sugar and Ve-Tsin
   (see page 151)
½ teaspoon soy sauce
1 teaspoon cornflour
1 dessertspoon cold water

After removing and discarding the stalks, cut the mushrooms in half. Slice the onion. Cut the pepper into 4-6 pieces and pick over the bean sprouts. Quarter 1 chestnut and leave the others whole. Slice the cucumber.
Heat the oil in the frying-pan. Cook the onion in it for ½ minute. Add the pepper, cook for ¼ minute, then add the bean sprouts, celery and cucumber. Add the mushrooms, chestnuts and bamboo shoots and cook for a minute or two, turning and tossing the vegetables.
Add the stock, seasonings and soy sauce and cook for 2 minutes. Stir in the cornflour, blended with the water, and boil for 1½ minutes.
Turn into a heated dish and serve.

LAN DOW
SNOW PEAS

Preparation time   2-3 minutes
Cooking time   5-6 minutes
To serve   2-3

You will need

4 oz. snow peas *
1 clove garlic
1 slice fresh ginger
1 tablespoon peanut oil
pinch each salt, sugar and Ve-Tsin
   (see page 151)
2-3 shakes white pepper
½ teaspoon ginger sherry (see page 151)
¼ pint (U.S. ⅝ cup) hot chicken stock

* These are also known as 'mange-tout', the pods as well as the peas being eaten.

String the peas, then wash and dry them. Crush the garlic and ginger. Heat the oil in a frying-pan. Add the garlic and ginger and cook until they are golden, then discard them. Add the peas and toss them about for a few seconds. Add the seasonings, ginger sherry and stock. Bring to the boil, stirring, and boil for 3-4 minutes. By this time, nearly all of the stock should have disappeared. Turn into a heated dish and serve.

CHOW NGAR CHOY
FRIED BEAN SPROUTS

(Illustrated in colour on page 113)

Preparation time   few minutes
Cooking time   6-7 minutes
To serve   4

You will need

8-10 tablespoons bean sprouts *
3 tablespoons very thin lean boiled ham
2 thin slices fresh ginger (see page 151)
1 small sliced onion
1½ dessertspoons peanut oil
pinch salt
tiny pinch each sugar and Ve-Tsin
   (see page 151)
½ teaspoon ginger sherry (see page 151)
1 teaspoon sesame oil
1 dessertspoon chicken stock

* Use bought bean sprouts or sprout them as directed on page 102.

Pick the bean sprouts over carefully, rinse and dry thoroughly. Cut the ham, ginger and onions in thin strips and have them ready separately.
Heat 1 dessertspoon oil in a frying-pan and cook the onion pieces in it for 2 minutes, moving them about. Add the ginger, cook for ½ minute, then add the bean sprouts and toss all about for 2 minutes. Add the salt, sugar and Ve-Tsin and continue to turn the mixture over and over. Finally, add the sherry, sesame oil and stock and heat through. Turn all into a heated serving dish.
Wipe out the pan. Heat the remaining oil in it then toss the thin strips of ham in it for ¼ minute. Place them on top of the bean sprouts and serve.

LAP CHU CHENG KWAR
CUCUMBER AND CHILLI

Preparation time   4-5 minutes
No cooking
To serve   2-3

You will need

1 whole or 6- to 7-inch piece cucumber
4 tablespoons white malt vinegar
1 tablespoon sugar
1 small chilli
pinch salt

Peel the cucumber. Cut it lengthwise into four and remove the seeds. Cut the cucumber diagonally into 1-inch pieces.
Blend together the vinegar and sugar. Add the crushed chilli and salt.
Leave for a few minutes then pour over the cucumber and serve.

Note

In place of the chilli, 3-4 drops of tabasco can be used.

CHOY FAR LUI
SPROUTING BROCCOLI

Preparation time   2-3 minutes
Cooking time   7-8 minutes
To serve   3

You will need

1 teaspoon sugar
1 tablespoon white malt vinegar
6 stalks sprouting broccoli
1 tablespoon peanut oil
1 clove garlic
1 thin slice fresh ginger
salt and Ve-Tsin (see page 151)
white pepper
½ teaspoon ginger sherry (see page 151)
3-4 tablespoons hot chicken stock
1 beaten egg

Blend together the sugar and vinegar and leave to rest.
Choose tender stalks of either green or purple sprouting broccoli. If the lower ends are a little hard, peel thin strips off them with a potato parer. Also crush the stem ends which will help them to absorb the stock and cook quickly. Drop the broccoli into boiling water for 5 minutes then drain well.
Heat the oil in a frying-pan. Add the crushed garlic and ginger, fry until golden and then discard both. Add the broccoli, pinch salt, pinch Ve-Tsin, few shakes pepper, sherry and stock and cook for 3-4 minutes, tossing the broccoli about.
Meanwhile, beat the egg and add a further tiny pinch each of salt and Ve-Tsin and a little white pepper. Trickle the egg over the broccoli while moving it about.
Finally, sprinkle the sweetened vinegar over all. Toss for a few seconds to heat through.
Turn into a heated dish and serve.

CHOW CHOY LUI
FRIED BRUSSELS SPROUTS

Preparation time   2 minutes
Cooking time   9 minutes
To serve   2

You will need

6 Brussels sprouts
1 crushed clove garlic
1 tablespoon peanut oil
4 tablespoons hot chicken stock
½ teaspoon soy sauce
pinch each salt, sugar and Ve-Tsin
  (see page 151)
½ teaspoon cornflour
1 dessertspoon water

The sprouts should be firm and compact. If small, they can be left whole but it is a good idea to choose larger ones and halve them *(see photograph)*. In either case, remove and discard any damaged outer leaves.

Drop them into boiling water and boil for 4 to 5 minutes, depending on their size. Drain them well. Lightly brown the garlic in the hot oil and then discard it. Add the sprouts to the oil and cook for 2 minutes, tossing and turning them.

Add the stock, soy sauce and seasonings and bring to the boil. Push the sprouts to one side of the pan and stir the cornflour, blended with the water, into the boiling liquid. Cook for 1½ minutes. Place the sprouts in a heated dish; pour the sauce over them and serve.

LAI YOW KAN CHOY
CELERY IN CREAM SAUCE

Preparation time   3-4 minutes
Cooking time   20-22 minutes
To serve   3

You will need

1 small celery heart
7 dessertspoons water
pinch each salt, sugar and Ve-Tsin
  (see page 151)
4 tablespoons top of milk
¾ teaspoon cornflour

Cook the celery in slightly salted boiling water for 20 minutes.

Place 6 dessertspoons of water and the seasonings in a small pan and bring to the boil. Add the milk and then the cornflour, blended with the remaining water, and boil for 1½ minutes.

Drain the celery and gently press out the remaining moisture in a linen cloth. Cut the celery into 6 pieces and arrange them in a heated serving dish. Spoon the sauce over them.

Fried Brussels sprouts

Celery in cream sauce

CHOW KAN CHOY

FRIED CELERY

Preparation time 3-4 minutes
Cooking time 7-8 minutes
To serve 2-3

You will need

6-7 tablespoons celery
1 clove garlic
1 slice fresh ginger
  (see page 151)
1 tablespoon peanut oil
pinch each salt, sugar and Ve-Tsin
  (see page 151)
2-3 shakes white pepper
½ teaspoon ginger sherry (see page 151)
¼ pint (U.S. ⅝ cup) hot chicken stock

For this dish, use the inner stalks (but not the heart) of celery.
Cut the stalks diagonally into 1-inch strips.
Crush the garlic and ginger.
Heat the oil in a frying-pan, cook the garlic and ginger in it until golden brown and then discard them.
Add to the pan the celery, seasonings, sherry and stock and cook for 5-6 minutes. The stock should almost disappear.
The celery will be cooked but still crisp. Turn into a heated dish and serve.

CHOW SAI YUNG CHOY

FRIED WATERCRESS

Preparation time 2-3 minutes
Cooking time 4-5 minutes
To serve 2-3

You will need

4 oz. watercress
1 dessertspoon peanut oil
1 crushed thin slice ginger (see page 151)
1 crushed clove garlic
4 tablespoons hot chicken stock
½ teaspoon ginger sherry (see page 151)
pinch each salt, sugar and Ve-Tsin
  (see page 151)
¼ teaspoon soy sauce
¼ teaspoon cornflour
1 dessertspoon cold water

Pick over the watercress, removing and discarding any discoloured or limp leaves, but do not trim the stalks unless they are very coarse.
Heat the oil and in it fry the ginger and garlic. When the latter is pale gold discard it.
Add the stock, sherry, watercress, seasonings and soy sauce, and stir while cooking for 1 minute.
Stir in the cornflour, blended with the water, and boil for 1½ minutes.
Turn into a heated dish and serve.

Fried watercress

JUK SUN MAR TAI TUNG GOO
FRIED BAMBOO SHOOTS, WATER CHESTNUTS AND CHINESE MUSHROOMS

Preparation time   5-6 minutes
Cooking time   3-4 minutes
To serve   3

You will need

3-4 tablespoons bamboo shoots
3-4 water chestnuts
2 Chinese mushrooms (see page 150)
1 crushed clove garlic
1 tablespoon peanut oil
3-4 roughly cut pieces of onion
¼ pint (U.S. ⅝ cup) hot chicken stock
pinch each salt, sugar and Ve-Tsin
   (see page 151)
½ teaspoon soy sauce
1 level teaspoon cornflour
1 dessertspoon cold water

Thinly slice the bamboo shoots. Halve or quarter the chestnuts. Slice the mushrooms, discarding the stalks.
Fry the garlic in the oil until golden and then discard it. Fry the pieces of onion for ¼ minute. Add the bamboo shoots, chestnuts and mushrooms and cook for ½ minute. Add the hot stock, the seasonings and the soy sauce. Bring to the boil.
Blend the cornflour with the water and stir it in. Boil for 1½ minutes.
Turn into a heated dish and serve.

BAT SAN HAI YUK
ASPARAGUS WITH CRAB SAUCE

Preparation time   3-4 minutes
Cooking time   10 minutes
To serve   2-3

You will need

9 tender asparagus spears
2 oz. cooked white crab meat
4 tablespoons hot chicken stock
pinch each pepper, salt and Ve-Tsin
   (see page 151)
few drops ginger sherry (see page 151)
few drops sesame oil
½ teaspoon cornflour
1 teaspoon water
1 beaten egg white
1 teaspoon peanut oil

Cut off and discard any woody ends of the asparagus and very thinly peel the remaining lower ends. Cut the asparagus into 1½- to 2-inch lengths. Drop them into very slightly salted boiling water and boil for 9-10 minutes while getting on with the crab sauce.
Flake the crab meat and have it ready.
Turn the stock, seasonings, sherry and sesame oil into a frying-pan and heat them through. Blend the cornflour with the water and add it. Cook for 1½ minutes. Add the crab meat and let the mixture come almost to the boil.
Remove from the heat and stir in the egg white beaten with the oil.
Turn the well drained asparagus into a heated dish and spoon the crab sauce over it.

Note

Canned or frozen crab meat is probably the easiest to prepare. If cooked fresh crab is used, do not include any of the dark meat.

CHEN CHOW KAI LAN
SPRING GREENS

Preparation time   3 minutes
Cooking time   3-4 minutes
To serve   3

You will need

4—6 oz. spring greens
1 thin slice fresh ginger *
1 crushed clove garlic
1 tablespoon peanut oil
½ teaspoon ginger sherry (see below)
¼ pint (U.S. ⅝ cup) hot chicken stock
pinch each salt, sugar and Ve-Tsin
  (see page 151)
¼ teaspoon soy sauce
¾ teaspoon cornflour
1 dessertspoon cold water

* This is different from dried root ginger as it is moist and almost juicy. It is usually cut into slices or shreds and either cooked in oil until a pale golden colour and then discarded or left in the dish with the other ingredients.

Wash, drain and cut the greens into suitable pieces.
Cut the ginger into thin strips.
Fry the garlic in the oil until golden and then discard it.
Add the greens, ginger, ginger sherry and stock and cook very quickly at a high heat for just under 2 minutes.
If, by this time, the stock is almost absorbed, add a little more.
Add the seasonings and soy sauce and bring to the boil.
Push the greens to one side of the pan and stir the cornflour, blended with the water, into the stock. Continue to stir while boiling for 1½ minutes. Turn into a heated serving dish.

Note

Brussels sprout tops can be cooked in the same way.

TO MAKE GINGER SHERRY

Cut 1-2 oz. fresh ginger into thin strips. Turn them into a bottle and cover with a warm brown sherry.
Leave the ginger to infuse in the sherry.
Then strain and use as directed.
For 2 oz. fresh ginger ½ bottle sherry will be the right amount to add.

Spring greens

Stuffed green sweet peppers

YEUNG CHING CHU
STUFFED GREEN SWEET PEPPERS

Preparation time   20 minutes
Cooking time   10 minutes
To serve   3

You will need

3 stumpy green peppers
6 oz. leg of pork (with some fat on it)
1 dessertspoon canned water chestnuts
1 dessertspoon canned bamboo shoots
salt, sugar and Ve-Tsin (see page 151)
1 teaspoon beaten egg
1-2 tablespoons peanut oil
¼ pint (U.S. ⅝ cup) hot chicken stock
¼ teaspoon soy sauce
¾ teaspoon cornflour
1 dessertspoon cold water

Cut a thin slice off the stem end of each pepper and remove the seeds, leaving the 'divisions' intact.
Very finely chop the pork, chestnuts and bamboo shoots. Mix them together. Add a pinch of salt, sugar and Ve-Tsin and the beaten egg and work them well in. Knead and throw the mixture as with dough when making bread.
Divide into three and fill each section of the pepper with a portion, gently pressing it in.
Get the oil very hot. Place the stuffed peppers in it, meat sides down, and fry for 5-6 minutes.
Add the stock, another pinch of salt, sugar and Ve-Tsin and soy sauce and cook for a further 3 minutes.

Blend the cornflour with the water and stir it in. Boil for 1½ minutes.
Arrange the peppers in a heated dish, spoon the sauce over them and serve.

GEE YUK DAI SUN
LEEKS AND PORK

Preparation time   about 6 minutes
Cooking time   6-8 minutes
To serve   2-3

You will need

2 tablespoons raw leg of pork
salt and Ve-Tsin (see page 151)
white pepper
1 teaspoon ginger sherry (see page 151)
few drops sesame oil
1 small teaspoon cornflour
1 teaspoon water
1 very thin slice fresh ginger
1 tablespoon peanut oil
4-5 tablespoons leeks *
¼ teaspoon sugar
3-5 tablespoons hot chicken stock

* The leeks should be cleaned and cut diagonally into 1-inch slices and separated.

Cut the pork into thin slices, diagonally. (This helps to retain their shape during the cooking). Place the slices in a basin with a good pinch salt, good pinch Ve-Tsin, a few shakes pepper, ½ teaspoon ginger sherry, sesame oil, cornflour and water.
Chop the ginger.
Heat the oil in a frying-pan and fry the ginger in it for ¼ minute.
Add the pork and fry it for 4 minutes. Add the leeks, another good pinch salt, good pinch Ve-Tsin, few shakes pepper, the remaining ginger sherry and a few drops sesame oil.
Add also the sugar and stock and cook for 2-3 minutes.
Turn into a heated dish and serve.

Note

There is hardly any liquid left when this dish is ready.

Onions and tomatoes in simple sauce

CHOW BOR CHOY
FRIED SPINACH

Preparation time   10 minutes
Cooking time   4-5 minutes
To serve   2-3

You will need

8 oz. spinach, stalks discarded
1 crushed clove garlic
1 tablespoon peanut oil
¼ pint (U.S. ⅝ cup) hot chicken stock
pinch each salt, sugar and Ve-Tsin
   (see page 151)
½ teaspoon soy sauce
¼ teaspoon cornflour
1 dessertspoon water

Turn spinach into a large basin of cold water so that it can float well. Plunge it up and down several times. Lift out into a colander and drain. Do this three times in all to make sure that all the grit has been removed. Lift out and drain thoroughly.
Fry the garlic in the hot oil until golden and then discard it. Add the spinach to the oil and cook it at high heat for 1 minute, tossing and turning it. Add the hot stock, seasoning and soy sauce and boil for 2 minutes. Finally, blend the cornflour with the water and stir it in. Boil for 1½ minutes. Turn into a heated dish and serve.

YUNG CHONG FAN KAY
ONION AND TOMATOES
IN SIMPLE SAUCE

Preparation time   3-4 minutes
Cooking time   8-9 minutes
To serve   2-3

You will need

1 medium-sized onion
2 tomatoes *
1 tablespoon peanut oil
pinch each salt, sugar and Ve-Tsin
   (see page 151)
½ teaspoon soy sauce
4 tablespoons hot chicken stock
¾ teaspoon cornflour
1 tablespoon water
1 onion 'flower' (see page 49)

* Choose firm and ripe tomatoes.

Roughly chop the onion. Cut the firm tomatoes into eighths and set aside. Heat the oil in a frying-pan and fry the onion in it for 4 minutes, tossing it about.
Add a pinch salt, pinch sugar, pinch Ve-Tsin, soy sauce and chicken stock and cook for a further 2 minutes.
Add the tomatoes and gently move them about so as not to break them up. Blend the cornflour with the water, stir it in and boil for 1½ minutes. Turn into a heated serving dish and garnish with the onion 'flower'.

Fried spinach

DIM SIN CHOP CHOY
SWEET-SOUR MIXED VEGETABLES

Preparation time 6-7 minutes
Cooking time 5-6 minutes
To serve 3

You will need

1 dessertspoon sugar
1 tablespoon white malt vinegar
1 medium-sized onion
1 tablespoon green sweet pepper
1 tablespoon celery
2-3 cauliflower fleurets
1 tablespoon leeks
1 tablespoon canned bamboo shoots
1 tablespoon canned water chestnuts
1 pea-sized piece garlic
1 pea-sized piece fresh ginger
1 tablespoon peanut oil
3-4 tablespoons onion
1 teaspoon ginger sherry (see page 151)
pinch each salt, sugar and Ve-Tsin
  (see page 151)
2-3 shakes white pepper
few drops sesame oil
3-4 tablespoons hot chicken stock

Add the sugar to the vinegar and leave to dissolve. Roughly cut up the pepper. Cut the celery into 1½-inch strips, ¼-inch wide. Cut the leeks into diagonal rounds, ¼-inch wide. Slice the bamboo shoots into diagonal strips and the chestnuts into strips.
Crush and chop the garlic and ginger.
Heat the oil in a frying-pan. Toss and cook the onion in it for 1 minute.
Turn the remaining vegetables, garlic and ginger, all at once, into the frying-pan and add the sherry, seasonings, sesame oil and stock.
Cook for 4-5 minutes, tossing the vegetables about. When nearly all the stock has evaporated, sprinkle the sweetened vinegar into the pan and stir for a few seconds to heat through.
Turn the mixture into a heated dish and serve at once.

CHOW SAN CHOY
COOKED COS LETTUCE

(Illustrated in colour on opposite page)

Preparation time 1-2 minutes
Cooking time ½-1 minute
To serve 2-3

You will need

6-8 cos lettuce leaves
¼ pint (U.S. ⅝ cup) chicken stock
peanut oil
soy sauce
pinch each salt and Ve-Tsin (see page 151)

Pick over and wash the lettuce leaves. Bring the stock, 1 dessertspoon oil, few drops soy sauce, salt and Ve-Tsin to the boil.
Drop the lettuce leaves into the liquid and cook for ½-1 minute.
Drain immediately.
Place on a suitable platter.
Mix together a few drops of soy sauce and peanut oil and spoon them over the lettuce.

Cos lettuce; barbecued pork; fried bean sprouts

Meat and vegetables on transparent noodles

NOODLES, RICE AND DUMPLINGS

MEIN; FAN; BOW

Since noodles, rice and dumplings are each based on flour, they are placed together in this section. If you can buy fresh noodles, there is no need to make your own — but, once you have made them, you will continue to do so. The recipe for noodle dough is given below.

All noodles mentioned in this section can be bought in any Chinese emporium.

But every kind of noodle you are ever likely to need can be bought from any shop specialising in oriental supplies.

Some varieties, like rice noodles, will have to be bought as their making at home is hardly practicable. Rice noodles, being very thin and delicate require scarcely any cooking. Failing fresh noodles, dried noodles can be bought from any of the stores and most grocers.

The dough of home-made noodles can also be used for steamed dumplings.

Crispy noodles and noodle 'nests' (see page 116) are specialities of the Chinese kitchen. They are well worth the care and dexterity they require.

Chinese rice to be served with fish and meat is small-grained, as a rule.

Today, some chefs prefer to use Carolina rice, which is long-grained. I myself use a non-stick pan for cooking rice so that it is beautifully dry with each grain separate. With such a pan, there is no waste.

DAN MIN

NOODLE DOUGH

Preparation time   20 minutes
Cooking time   as required

You will need

1 lb. plain hard flour *
good pinch salt
4 eggs
cold water

* Hard flour, which contains a generous proportion of gluten, is the flour used for bread.
An 'all-purpose' flour is also suitable but a light cake flour is not.

This is the basic recipe for noodles. The number of servings depends on the dish in which the noodles are used.

Sift the flour and salt on to a pastry board.

Make a depression in the centre and drop in the eggs and a little cold water.

Gradually work the mixture together with the handle of a wooden spoon to form a very stiff dough.

Gather it into a ball.

To prevent it sticking, dust the board with flour or cornflour and knead the dough very well with the heels of the hands until firm but pliable and close textured and dry rather than moist.

Roll out the dough in a long sheet, less than $\frac{1}{8}$ inch thick.

Fold over and over and cut into thin strips about $\frac{1}{4}$ inch in width.

The length of the noodles depends on the space you have in which to roll out the dough in the first place.

GAI SEE JAR MIN
CRISPY NOODLES WITH CHICKEN AND VEGETABLES

Preparation time   4-5 minutes excluding noodles
Cooking time   6 minutes
To serve   2

You will need

¼ recipe noodles (see page 115)
peanut oil
2 tablespoons raw chicken
1 medium-sized onion
1 tablespoon raw carrot
1 tablespoon green sweet pepper
1 tablespoon canned bamboo shoots
3 oz. bean sprouts
¼ pint (U.S. ⅝ cup) hot chicken stock
pinch each salt, sugar and Ve-Tsin
  (see page 151)
½ teaspoon soy sauce
1 small teaspoon cornflour
1 tablespoon cold water

Make the noodles as directed on page 115, using a quarter of the quantities. Make a 'nest' of the noodles as follows: Have a 5-inch wire frying basket in one hand. Gather the ends of the noodles in the fingers of the other, letting them extend themselves for their full length. Let the other ends of the noodles fall into the basket, easing and turning them so that they line the basket in neat

Crispy noodles with chicken and vegetables

rounds to form a 'nest'. Lower the basket into fairly warm oil and at once remove and drain it. Set this aside while preparing the chicken and vegetables.

Slice the chicken, onion, carrot, pepper and bamboo shoots in thin strips and keep them separate. Pick over the sprouts. Heat 1 tablespoon oil in the frying-pan. Add and cook the onion for ½ minute. Add the bean sprouts and cook for 1 minute. Add the chicken and remaining vegetables and cook for a further 2 minutes, tossing all about. Stir in the stock, seasonings and soy sauce and cook for 1 minute or so. Get the oil for deep frying hot enough to cook the noodles and colour them in 3-4 minutes — that is, when a dried slice of raw potato rises in 4 seconds when dropped into the oil. Lower the basket with its noodle 'nest' into the oil and raise the temperature to make up for its being lowered when the noodles go into it. Cook for 3-4 minutes.

Meanwhile blend the cornflour with the water, stir it into the other mixture and boil for 1½ minutes. Turn all into a heated dish and place the well drained noodle 'nest' on top.

SUB GUM WUI MIN
NOODLES WITH MIXED MEATS AND PRAWNS

Preparation time   10 minutes
Cooking time   6-8 minutes
To serve   2-3

You will need

2 oz. long life noodles
peanut oil
1 oz. raw pig's liver
1 oz. raw pig's heart
1 Pacific prawn
3-4 small heart of lettuce leaves
1-2 Chinese mushrooms (see page 150)
1 crushed clove garlic
1 teaspoon ginger sherry (see page 151)
¼ pint (U.S. ⅝ cup) chicken stock
pinch each salt, sugar and Ve-Tsin
  (see page 151)
½ teaspoon soy sauce
1 teaspoon cornflour
1 tablespoon cold water

Drop the noodles into boiling water and cook for 4-5 minutes. Drain well. Sprinkle with a few drops of oil to keep them separate.

Cut the meats into thin slices and the prawn into

Noodles with mixed meats and prawns

slightly thicker ones. Break the lettuce leaves into suitable pieces and slice the mushrooms. Place them in another dish.

Heat 1 tablespoon oil in a frying-pan. Cook the garlic in it until golden and then discard it.

Add the meats and prawn and fry for 3-4 minutes.

Add the sherry and stock and cook for 1 minute.

Add the lettuce, mushrooms, seasonings and soy sauce. Boil rapidly, stirring together. Finally, blend the cornflour with the water, stir it in and cook for $1\frac{1}{2}$ minutes, still stirring.

Turn into a heated dish and serve.

JING CHOW MEIN
FRIED SOFT NOODLES

(Illustrated in colour on page 124)

Preparation time   30 minutes
Cooking time   7-8 minutes
To serve   2

You will need

$\frac{1}{4}$ recipe noodle dough (see page 115)
1 tablespoon peanut oil
1 slice onion
$\frac{1}{4}$ pint (U.S. $\frac{5}{8}$ cup) chicken stock
good pinch each salt, sugar and Ve-Tsin (see page 151)
$\frac{1}{2}$ teaspoon soy sauce
1 teaspoon cornflour
1 dessertspoon cold water
2 onion 'flowers' (see page 49)

Boil the noodles for 10 minutes then drain them well.

Heat the oil and toss the onion in it for $\frac{1}{2}$ minute.

Add the drained cooked noodles and turn them over and over to coat them with the oil.

Add the stock, seasonings and soy sauce and cook for 4-5 minutes.

Blend the cornflour with the water and stir it in, adding a little extra stock, if necessary. Boil for $1\frac{1}{2}$ minutes.

Turn all into a heated serving dish and garnish with the onion 'flowers'.

Note

You may be able to buy fresh egg noodles. In this case, proceed as above. If you buy packaged egg noodles, they will require a little longer cooking.

GAI PIN DAN MIN
EGG NOODLES AND CHICKEN

Preparation time   8 minutes (including boiling the noodles)
Cooking time   6-7 minutes
To serve   2-3

You will need

2 tablespoons raw breast of chicken
salt and Ve-Tsin (see page 151)
pepper
$\frac{1}{2}$ teaspoon ginger sherry (see page 151)
few drops sesame oil
1 finely chopped slice fresh ginger
1 finely chopped clove garlic
1 round egg noodles
3 teaspoons peanut oil
hot chicken stock
$\frac{1}{2}$ teaspoon cornflour
1 teaspoon water

Cut the raw breast of chicken diagonally into thin slices. Put them in a basin. Add a pinch each salt and Ve-Tsin, few shakes pepper, sherry, sesame oil, ginger and garlic and work them all well together. Drop the noodles into boiling water, cook for 3-4 minutes. Rinse in cold water and drain well.

Heat 2 teaspoons peanut oil in a frying-pan. Add the prepared chicken and toss it about for 2-3 minutes. Add $\frac{1}{4}$ pint (U.S. $\frac{5}{8}$ cup) chicken stock and cook for 1 minute. Blend the cornflour with the water, stir it in and cook for $1\frac{1}{2}$ minutes.

Reheat the noodles in 4-5 tablespoons chicken stock, 1 teaspoon peanut oil and further seasonings. Drain. Place in a heated dish and cut with scissors into suitable lengths. Turn the hot chicken mixture on top and serve at once.

YEUNG CHOW CHO MIN

NOODLES WITH MIXED MEATS, PRAWNS AND VEGETABLES

Preparation time   8-10 minutes
Cooking time   6-8 minutes
To serve   2

You will need

1-2 oz. long life-noodles
peanut oil
1½ tablespoons cooked chicken
1½ tablespoons roast lean pork
1½ tablespoons cooked prawns
1 tablespoon canned bamboo shoots
½ tablespoon green pepper
1 medium-sized onion
½ tablespoon carrot
4 tablespoons bean sprouts
¼ pint (U.S. ⅝ cup) hot chicken stock
tiny pinch pepper
pinch each salt, sugar and Ve-Tsin
   (see page 151)
½ teaspoon soy sauce
1 small teaspoon cornflour
1 tablespoon cold water

Drop the noodles into boiling water and boil for 4-5 minutes. Drain well. Sprinkle with a drop or two of oil to prevent them sticking together.
Cut the meats, bamboo shoots, pepper, onion and carrot into thin strips. Pick over the bean sprouts.

Noodles with mixed meats, prawns and vegetables

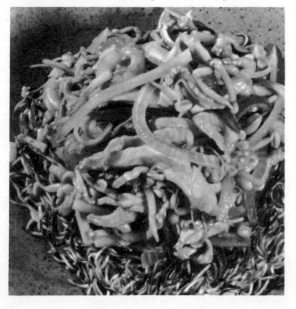

Heat 1 tablespoon oil in a frying-pan. Add the noodles and turn them over and over in it, adding a little more oil, if necessary. Add the vegetables and turn them over and over. Add the stock, seasonings, chicken, pork and prawns and mix all together. Add the soy sauce. Finally, blend the cornflour with the water, stir it into the boiling mixture and cook for 1½ minutes.
Turn into a heated dish and serve.

GEUNG SUNG MIN

GINGER NOODLES

Preparation time   5-6 minutes
Cooking time   20-25 minutes
To serve   2-3

You will need

3 oz. long-life noodles
¾ pint (U.S. 1⅞ cup) hot chicken stock
3 teaspoons peanut oil
3 large thin slices fresh ginger (see page 151)
2 spring onions
1 clove garlic
pinch each salt and Ve-Tsin (see page 151)
1 teaspoon ginger sherry (see page 151)
few drops sesame oil
½ teaspoon soy sauce
½ teaspoon cornflour
1 teaspoon water

Drop the noodles into ½ pint (U.S. 1¼ cups) boiling stock and 1 teaspoon peanut oil and boil them until soft, moving them about with chopsticks or the handle of a wooden spoon to keep them separate. Meanwhile, prepare the dressing so that no time is lost in the final stages of the dish. Cut the ginger into thin strips. Cut the spring onions in 4-5 long strips and then into match stick sizes. Place them ready.
Heat 2 teaspoons peanut oil in a frying-pan. Add the crushed clove of garlic, cook until it becomes a pale gold colour and then discard it. Add ¼ pint (U.S. ⅝ cup) chicken stock and the ginger and cook for 1 minute. Add the seasonings, ginger sherry, sesame oil, soy sauce and onions and cook for 2 minutes. Blend the cornflour with the water and stir it in. Cook for 1½ minutes.
By this time, the noodles should be ready. Turn a little cold water on to them and drain well. Transfer them to a heated dish and cut them with scissors into the lengths you wish.

Pour the ginger sauce over the noodles, work it well in and then serve.

YEUNG CHOW WOR MIN

NOODLES WITH VEGETABLES AND MEATS

Preparation time   20 minutes
Cooking time   8 minutes
To serve   3-4

You will need

2 oz. long life noodles
2 Chinese mushrooms (see page 150)
4-5 slices canned bamboo shoots
2 tablespoons pig's liver
1 chicken liver
2 tablespoons lean roast pork
2 tablespoons pig's heart
4-5 slices canned awabi
2 tablespoons peanut oil
$\frac{1}{4}$ pint (U.S. $\frac{5}{8}$ cup) chicken stock
good pinch each salt, sugar and Ve-Tsin
  (see page 151)
1 teaspoon ginger sherry (see page 151)
$\frac{1}{2}$ teaspoon soy sauce
2-3 sprigs watercress
1 good teaspoon cornflour
1 tablespoon cold water
1 onion 'flower' (see page 49)

Drop noodles into boiling water and boil for 7-10 minutes.
Slice mushrooms. Cut bamboo shoots into not-too-thin strips. Cut the livers, pork and heart into thin strips and the awabi into wider ones. Place each separate from the others on a large plate. Heat 1 tablespoon of the oil. Lower the drained noodles into in and turn them around as they cook for 3-4 minutes. Arrange them in a circle in a heated dish and keep them hot.
Add the remaining oil to the pan and cook the mixed meats in it for 2 minutes. Add the mushrooms, bamboo shoots, awabi and stock and bring to the boil. Next, add the seasonings, sherry, soy sauce and watercress and boil for 1 minute.
Blend the cornflour with the water and stir it into the boiling mixture. Continue to stir while cooking for $1\frac{1}{2}$ minutes. Place the mixture on top of the hot noodles and garnish with the onion 'flower'.

YUK YIN FAN SEE

TRANSPARENT NOODLES WITH MEAT BALLS

Preparation time   6-7 minutes
Cooking time   13-14 minutes
To serve   2-3

You will need

$1\frac{1}{2}$-2 oz. transparent noodles
peanut oil
6 oz. raw pork with a little fat in it
1 dessertspoon canned water chestnuts
1 dessertspoon canned bamboo shoots
pinch each salt, sugar and Ve-Tsin
  (see page 151)
1 crushed small clove garlic
1 crushed thin slice fresh ginger
1 finely chopped spring onion
1 good teaspoon beaten egg
self-raising flour
$\frac{1}{4}$ pint (U.S. $\frac{5}{8}$ cup) chicken stock
finely chopped green of 1 spring onion

BATTER

4 tablespoons self-raising flour
7-8 tablespoons water

Drop the noodles into boiling water for $\frac{1}{2}$ minute. Drain them. Heat 1 tablespoon peanut oil in a frying-pan. Drop the noodles into it, toss them about for $\frac{1}{4}$ minute and drain again.
Cut the pork, chestnuts and bamboo shoots into pieces then chop them finely. Add the seasonings. Heat 1 teaspoon peanut oil in a frying-pan. Fry the garlic and ginger in it until a golden colour and then discard them. Add the onion to the pan and cook it for 1 minute, without colouring it. Add it to the meat mixture, then add the beaten egg and beat well and knead to combine the flavours evenly. Form the mixture into balls the size of hazel-nuts, drop them into self-raising flour and work it into them between the palms of the hands. Make a thin batter with the self-raising flour and the water. Beat well, leave for a few minutes, then roll the meat balls in the batter. Drop the balls into hot deep oil (375°F. or 190°C.) and cook till a warm gold colour. Lift out and drain. Bring the chicken stock to the boil. Gently boil the meat balls in it for 5-6 minutes. Add the noodles and heat through.
Turn into a heated dish. Garnish with the onion green and serve.

CHUN GON WUI MIN
NOODLES AND CHICKEN LIVERS

Preparation time   20-25 minutes
Cooking time   6-8 minutes
To serve   2-3

You will need

2 oz. long-life noodles
2 Chinese mushrooms (see page 150)
4 raw chicken livers
4 thin slices fresh ginger (see page 151)
4 slices canned bamboo shoots
few cos lettuce leaves
1 onion
2 tablespoons peanut oil
1 crushed clove garlic
salt, sugar and Ve-Tsin (see page 151)
$\frac{1}{4}$ pint (U.S. $\frac{5}{8}$ cup) chicken stock
$\frac{1}{2}$ teaspoon ginger sherry (see page 151)
$\frac{1}{2}$ teaspoon soy sauce
1 teaspoon cornflour
1 tablespoon cold water

Drop the noodles into boiling water and boil them for 7-10 minutes while preparing the remaining ingredients.
Slice the mushrooms. Slice the livers. Cut 3 slices of ginger into thin strips and the bamboo shoots into wider ones. Cut the lettuce into 2-inch pieces and slice the onion. Place these separately on a plate.

Noodles and chicken livers

Crush the remaining slice of ginger and heat 1 tablespoon of oil in the frying-pan and cook the garlic and ginger in it until pale gold. Discard them. Fry the drained noodles in the pan, adding a tiny pinch of salt, sugar and Ve-Tsin and stir them into the shape of the dish to be used. Turn them into it and keep them hot.
Wipe out the pan and add the remaining oil to it. Quickly fry the sliced onion for a minute then add the mushrooms and livers and toss them about. Follow immediately with the ginger, bamboo shoots and lettuce. Add the stock, sherry and another pinch of each of the seasonings and soy sauce and stir all together.
Blend the cornflour with the water, add it and stir while boiling for a further 1$\frac{1}{2}$ minutes.
Carefully turn this mixture on to the hot noodles.

CHOW YUK SUNG
MEAT AND VEGETABLES ON TRANSPARENT NOODLES
(Illustrated in colour on page 114)

Preparation time   8-9 minutes
Cooking time   6 minutes
To serve   2-3

You will need

1 tablespoon finely chopped lean pork
1 dessertspoon chopped prawns
1 dessertspoon chopped canned water
  chestnuts
1 chopped Chinese mushroom (see page 150)
1 dessertspoon chopped canned bamboo shoots
1$\frac{1}{2}$ tablespoons cooked peas
2 oz. transparent noodles
peanut oil
1 crushed clove garlic
1 chopped slice onion
pinch each salt, sugar and Ve-Tsin (see page 151)
$\frac{1}{2}$ teaspoon soy sauce
$\frac{1}{2}$ teaspoon sesame oil
2 tablespoons stock
$\frac{1}{2}$ beaten egg

Prepare the pork, prawns and vegetables and have the peas ready.
Drop the transparent noodles into boiling water and cook them for less than a minute. Drain and set them aside.
Heat 1 tablespoon of oil in a frying-pan. Fry the garlic in it to a pale gold colour and then discard it. Add the onion and fry it for $\frac{1}{2}$ minute, then add the pork, prawns, chestnuts, mushroom and

bamboo shoots. Move them about for 3-4 minutes until dry.

Add the seasonings, soy sauce, sesame oil, stock and egg and cook, stirring, for $\frac{1}{4}$ minute. Finally,add the peas and heat them through.

Meanwhile, cook the drained noodles in deep oil for less than a minute. Drain them, arrange them in a heated serving dish and turn the meat mixture on top.

KAY JOP MIN
FUKIEN NOODLES

Preparation time   5-6 minutes
Cooking time   20-25 minutes
To serve   2-3

You will need

3 oz. long-life noodles
$\frac{3}{4}$ pint (U.S. $1\frac{7}{8}$ cups) hot chicken stock
3 teaspoons peanut oil
1 tomato, skinned and seeded
2 spring onions
1 clove garlic
1 small dessertspoon tomato ketchup
pinch each salt and Ve-Tsin (see page 151)
$\frac{1}{2}$ teaspoon ginger sherry (see page 151)
few drops sesame oil
$\frac{1}{2}$ teaspoon soy sauce
1 small teaspoon cornflour
1 teaspoon water

Drop the noodles into $\frac{1}{2}$ pint (U.S. $1\frac{1}{4}$ cups) boiling chicken stock and 1 teaspoon peanut oil and cook until soft, moving them about with chopsticks or the handle of a wooden spoon to keep them separate. Cut the skinned and seeded tomato into fairly fine pieces. Cut the onions into thin lengths and then into match stick pieces. Heat 2 teaspoons peanut oil in a frying-pan and fry the crushed clove of garlic in it until a pale gold colour, then discard it.

Add the $\frac{1}{4}$ pint (U.S. $\frac{5}{8}$ cup) hot chicken stock, the tomato and the ketchup and cook for 1 minute. Add the onions, seasonings, sherry, sesame oil and soy sauce and cook for 2 minutes. Blend the cornflour with the water, add it and cook for $1\frac{1}{2}$ minutes. By this time, the noodles should be ready.

Add a little cold water to them, drain at once and turn them into a heated dish. Cut them into 'workable' lengths with a pair of scissors. Pour the tomato sauce over them and serve at once.

YUNG CHOW MEI FUN
FRIED RICE NOODLES WITH SHREDDED CHICKEN

Preparation time   6-7 minutes
Cooking time   8-9 minutes
To serve   3-4

You will need

1 tablespoon Chinese mushrooms
  (see page 150)
1 tablespoon green sweet pepper
2 tablespoons bean sprouts
2 tablespoons canned bamboo shoots
3 dessertspoons peanut oil
1 chopped small onion
4 tablespoons strips breast of chicken
2 tablespoons shelled cooked prawns
$\frac{1}{2}$ teaspoon ginger sherry (see page 151)
few drops sesame oil
$\frac{1}{2}$ teaspoon soy sauce
pinch each salt, sugar and Ve-Tsin
  (see page 151)
$\frac{1}{2}$ pint (U.S. $1\frac{1}{4}$ cups) chicken stock
2 oz. thin rice noodles
1 teaspoon cornflour
1 tablespoon water
watercress garnish

Cut the mushrooms, sweet pepper and bamboo shoots into strips and pick over the bean sprouts. Heat 2 dessertspoons of peanut oil in a frying-pan and fry the onion in it for 1-2 minutes.

Add the chicken breast and cook for 1-2 minutes. Add the prawns and mushrooms and cook for 1-2 minutes, then add the pepper, bean sprouts and bamboo shoots and let all cook for a further 2-3 minutes.

Add the sherry, sesame oil, soy sauce, seasonings and stock and cook together for 2-3 minutes.

Meanwhile drop the noodles into boiling water for $\frac{1}{2}$ minute.

Drain, rinse in cold water and drain very well again.

Heat the remaining oil and toss the noodles in it until heated through, and coated with the oil to the glistening stage, but not coloured. Stir the cornflour, blended with the water, into the chicken mixture and boil for $1\frac{1}{2}$ minutes. Turn the mixture into a heated serving dish, top with the noodles and garnish with watercress.

YOUNG CHOW MEI FIN

FRIED RICE NOODLES WITH PRAWNS AND CHICKEN

(Illustrated in colour on opposite page)

Preparation time 6-8 minutes
Cooking time about 10 minutes
To serve 2-3

You will need

5 dessertspoons peanut oil
1 sliced small onion
1 tablespoon thinly sliced celery
1 tablespoon sliced green sweet pepper
1 tablespoon bean sprouts
salt, sugar and Ve-Tsin (see page 151)
dash soy sauce
1 oz. Chinese rice noodles
1 tablespoon cooked prawns
1 tablespoon sliced roast chicken
1 tablespoon sliced canned bamboo shoots
1 Chinese mushroom, cut into strips
   (see page 150)
1 teaspoon sesame oil
4-5 tablespoons chicken stock
1 teaspoon ginger sherry (see page 151)
$\frac{1}{2}$-$\frac{3}{4}$ teaspoon cornflour
1 tablespoon water
watercress

Heat 2 dessertspoons of the oil and cook the onion in it for 2 minutes, without colouring it. Add the celery, green pepper and bean sprouts at intervals of 1 minute and season very lightly with a tiny pinch each of salt, sugar and Ve-Tsin and the soy sauce. Toss about for 1 minute and remove to a hot plate. Meanwhile drop the rice noodles into boiling water for 1 minute and drain them well. Wipe out the frying-pan. Add another 2 dessertspoons of peanut oil and heat it. Add the prawns, chicken, bamboo shoots and mushroom and heat through. Add another tiny pinch each of the seasonings together with the sesame oil. Add the stock and sherry and then the first vegetables. Boil up. Stir in the cornflour blended with the water and boil for 1½ minutes. Turn the mixture into a heated serving dish. Wipe out the pan again and heat the remaining oil in it. Toss the drained boiled noodles in it until heated through and glistening.
Place on top of the savoury mixture and garnish with watercress.

CHOP CHOY CHOW MIN

FRIED NOODLES WITH VEGETABLES

Preparation time 10 minutes
Cooking time 15-20 minutes
To serve 3

You will need

3 oz. long-life noodles
7 teaspoons peanut oil
1 roughly cut small onion
1 tablespoon celery, cut in ½-inch slices
1 tablespoon sliced green sweet pepper
1 sliced Chinese mushroom (see page 150)
2 small unopened fresh mushrooms, each
   cut into 4-6 pieces
1 tablespoon canned water chestnuts, cut
   in ½-inch slices
1 tablespoon canned bamboo shoots, cut
   in ½-inch pieces
¼ pint (U.S. ⅝ cup) hot chicken stock
salt, sugar and Ve-Tsin (see page 151)
few shakes pepper
½ teaspoon soy sauce
½ teaspoon ginger sherry (see page 151)
few drops sesame oil
½ teaspoon cornflour
1 teaspoon water
handful bean sprouts (see page 102)

Cook the noodles in boiling water and teaspoon peanut oil until soft.
Drain, rest on a sieve.
Heat 4 teaspoons peanut oil in a frying-pan. Toss and cook the onion in it for 1 minute. Add the celery and toss and cook it for 1 minute. Next add the green pepper. Cook for ½ minute. Add the Chinese and fresh mushrooms (the latter washed but unpeeled) and cook them a further ½ minute. Follow with the chestnuts, bamboo shoots, pinch each salt, sugar and Ve-Tsin, the soy sauce, ginger sherry and sesame oil. Blend the cornflour with the water; stir it into the vegetables and boil for 1½ minutes. Heat a further 2 teaspoons peanut oil in another pan. Turn the picked-over bean sprouts and the noodles into it and toss them about. Add a pinch more of the seasonings.
When the mixture is really hot, turn it into a heated dish, top with the mixed vegetables and serve at once.

Special fried rice noodles with shredded chicken

Fried soft noodles

JAR JUNG MIN

SOFT NOODLES WITH HOT VEGETABLE DRESSING

Preparation time   10 minutes
Cooking time   5-6 minutes
To serve   2-3

You will need

1 tablespoon green onion
1 tablespoon canned bamboo shoots
1 clove garlic
1 slice fresh ginger
2 tablespoons Szechwan cabbage
   (see page 79)
5-10 dried chillis
1 dessertspoon peanut oil
hot chicken stock
pinch each sugar and Ve-Tsin
   (see page 151)
few shakes pepper
½ teaspoon ginger sherry (see page 151)
few drops sesame oil
2 tablespoons tomato ketchup
3 oz. parboiled long-life noodles
1 teaspoon cornflour
1 tablespoon water

Chop the onion, bamboo shoots, garlic and ginger and have them ready, each separate from the others.
Place the cabbage in a pan with cold water to cover. Bring to the boil, boil for 3 minutes. Drain, rinse, drain again and have ready.
Chop the chillis. It might be as well here to start with 5 rather than 10 and to work up to the larger number as one proceeds, as the chillis are very fiery.
Heat the peanut oil in a frying-pan and cook the onion for 1 minute, moving it about. Add the bamboo shoots, cabbage and chillis. Cover with the stock and cook for 3 minutes.
Add the seasonings, sherry, sesame oil and, lastly, the chopped garlic and ginger and the tomato ketchup.
If the liquid has evaporated too much, add a little more hot stock.
Add the noodles and cook until they are soft, stirring them about to keep them separate.
Blend the cornflour with the water, stir it in and boil for 1½ minutes. Season further, if necessary.

LAP CHUNG FAN

STEAMED RICE AND CHINESE SAUSAGE

Preparation time   3-4 minutes
Cooking time   30-35 minutes
To serve   3

You will need

8 oz. long-grained rice
2 Chinese dried sausages (see page 150)
water

The rice can be the best Patna or Carolina. Very well wash the rice. Place it in a bowl and let cold water run into it until the water is clear. Drain. Wipe the sausages with a hot damp cloth.
Turn the rice into a pan and cover it with cold water to a depth of 1 inch above the rice.
Bring to the boil. Reduce the heat. When most of the water has evaporated, place the sausages on top of the rice. Reduce the heat as low as possible. Cover the rice and sausages and steam for 20 minutes. Remove the sausages. With a very sharp knife, cut them diagonally into very thin slices to produce longish ovals.
Turn the rice into a heated dish. Arrange the slices of sausage on top and serve at once.

GING FAN

PLAIN STEAMED RICE

Preparation time   2-3 minutes
Cooking time   40 minutes
To serve   2

You will need

2 heaped tablespoons long-grained rice
6 tablespoons water

Wash the rice very well. Turn it into a basin with the water. Together they should reach no more than a quarter way up the basin. Place in the steamer and steam for 40 minutes.

Note

There is neither salt nor stock in this rice. The way of serving it is to place each portion in a bowl and take it to table to accompany fish, meat or poultry, each in mouth-sized pieces and already in its own sauce.

NGOW YUK SHA HO FUN

RICE STICKS WITH BEEF

Preparation time 12 minutes
Cooking time 8-9 minutes
To serve • 2-3

You will need

2 oz. rice sticks
3 tablespoons rump steak
2-3 lettuce leaves
1 spring onion
2 tablespoons peanut oil
1 crushed clove garlic
1 slice fresh ginger (see page 151)
pinch each salt, sugar and Ve-Tsin
    (see page 151)
½ teaspoon ginger sherry (see page 151)
¼ pint (U.S. ⅝ cup) chicken stock
¾ teaspoon cornflour
1 tablespoon water

Drop the rice sticks (wide rice noodles) into boiling water and boil for 7-10 minutes. Drain well and put aside. Cut the steak into very thin smallish slices. Break the lettuce into fair-sized pieces and cut the onion into 1-inch lengths. Heat a tablespoon of the oil in a frying-pan. Add the rice sticks and, as they cook for several minutes, move them about and form them into an oval shape. Turn them into a heated oval dish and keep hot.

Wipe out the pan. Add and heat the remaining oil,

Rice sticks with beef

cook the garlic and ginger in it to a brown tone and discard them. Add the steak and cook it for 2 minutes. Remove to a heated dish and keep hot. To the same pan with, if necessary, a little more oil, add the lettuce, onion, seasonings, sherry and stock and cook for 1 minute. Add the cornflour, blended with the water, and stir while cooking for 1½ minutes.

Add the meat to the hot stock and at once pour the mixture over the hot rice sticks and serve.

CUP DAI JUCK

CREAMY SOUPY RICE

Preparation time few minutes
Cooking time 15 minutes
To serve 2

You will need

¼ pint (U.S. ⅝ cup) rich strong chicken stock
1 chicken stock cube
1 tablespoon raw pig's kidney
1 tablespoon raw pig's heart
1 tablespoon raw pig's liver
1 tablespoon raw lean pork
3 oz. raw rice
2 pints (U.S. 5 cups) water
tiny pinch pepper
salt to taste
½ teaspoon Ve-Tsin (see page 151)
1 dessertspoon sesame or peanut oil
½ teaspoon cornflour
1 tablespoon water
1 teaspoon finely chopped green from
    spring onion

Wash the rice. Cut the meats into very thin strips and keep them separate. Boil the rice in the water for a few minutes. Add the stock, strengthened with the chicken stock cube. Add the meats separately so that they do not mix, then add the seasonings and oil. Cook gently for a further 10 minutes. Blend the cornflour with the water, stir it in and boil for 1½ minutes. Top with the green of the onion.
This is a kind of rich rice gruel with meats.

VARIATIONS

Sometimes, transparent noodles (about ½ oz.) are added to the soup. Cook them in boiling water for ¼ minute, then drain and add them.
If poached eggs are used, allow 1 per person. Have

Creamy soupy rice

Fried rice with egg

the boiling hot soup in a tureen. Crack and drop the eggs into it, leave for 3 minutes and serve. In this case, the meats may be omitted.

GAI DAN CHOW FAN

FRIED RICE WITH EGG

Preparation time   5 minutes
Cooking time   5 minutes
To serve   2-3

You will need

1 dessertspoon peanut oil
4-6 oz. cold boiled rice
pinch each salt and Ve-Tsin (see page 151)
½ teaspoon soy sauce
2 chopped spring onions
1 beaten egg
2 tablespoons cooked peas

Heat the oil in the frying-pan. Add the rice and, with the back of a large spoon or ladle, break up any lumps to separate the grains and coat them with the oil.
Stir in the seasonings and soy sauce.
Add the onions and cook them for 1 minute. Pour in the egg and break it up into small segments as it cooks. Add the peas and cook further just long enough to heat them through.
Transfer to a heated dish and serve.
The accompanying sauces are plum, mustard and chilli.

GAI TONG FAN

RICE COOKED IN CHICKEN STOCK

Preparation time   3-4 minutes
Cooking time   20-25 minutes
To serve   2-3

You will need

4 oz. long-grained rice
2 tablespoons raw chicken fat
1 clove garlic
rich chicken stock *

* If chicken stock is not available use 2 chicken cubes and water.

Wash the rice very well, rubbing it between the fingers. Drain and rinse until the water is clear. Drain thoroughly.
Cut the chicken fat into smallish pieces and fry them until only small brown crispy bits remain. Remove them.
Add the crushed clove of garlic and the rice and toss it about to coat it with the fat, without colouring it. Remove and discard the garlic.
Add cold chicken stock to a depth above the rice of 1½ times that of the rice. Bring to the boil and boil fairly fast without stirring.
When the stock has almost been absorbed by the rice, lower the heat and continue to cook until the rice is dry. It should be ready in 20-25 minutes.

Note
This rice is served with any chicken dish.

BARK BOW FAN
'EIGHT JEWEL' RICE

Preparation time　5-6 minutes
Cooking time　　6-8 minutes
To serve　　　　3

You will need

1 tablespoon peanut oil
3 dessertspoons chopped spring onion
2 tablespoons diced cooked lean pork
1 tablespoon diced cooked chicken
2 tablespoons shelled cooked prawns
6 oz. cooked rice
1 raw egg
1 tablespoon cooked peas
pinch each salt and Ve-Tsin (see page 151)
1 teaspoon soy sauce

Make the oil very hot. Fry 2 dessertspoons of onion in it for ¼ minute, tossing it about. Add the meats and prawns and give them 1 minute. Add the rice and heat through for 2-3 minutes, moving it about to break down any lumps.
Break in the egg and mix it in thoroughly but lightly (the rice must not be made mushy) for ½-1 minute. Add the peas, seasonings and soy sauce and heat through, stirring to mix well.
Finally, add the remaining finely chopped spring onion.
Turn into a heated dish and serve.

Eight jewel rice

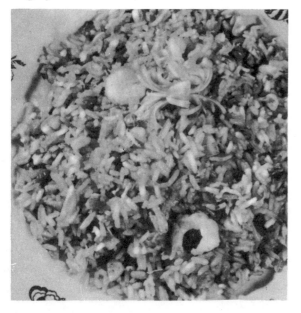

NGOW YUK JUCK
'SOUPY' RICE WITH BEEF

Preparation time　6-8 minutes
Cooking time　　3 hours
To serve　　　　2-3

You will need

2 tablespoons pudding (round) rice
1 piece tangerine peel (1 inch in diameter)
1 slice fresh ginger
peanut oil
water
6 oz. raw rump steak
1 teaspoon cornflour
pinch each salt and Ve-Tsin (see page 151)
½ teaspoon ginger sherry (see page 151)
1 oz. rice noodles

Well wash the rice. Turn it into a 3-pint saucepan. (If you have a non-stick pan, use it). Add the tangerine peel, ginger, 2 teaspoons peanut oil and 2 pints (U.S. 5 cups) water. Cover and very slowly cook for 3 hours, stirring occasionally to bring the rice up to the surface.
While the rice is cooking, finely chop the steak. Add the cornflour, blended with 1 dessertspoon water, the seasonings and sherry. Stir together and have ready.
In hot peanut oil deep-fat fry the rice noodles for ½ minute, keeping them submerged in the oil with a flattish perforated ladle. Lift out, drain and mix with the raw meat.
At the last minute, remove the peel and ginger from the rice. Stir the meat-noodle mixture into the 'soupy' rice and cook for 1 minute only.

Note

This dish is excellent for people with weak digestions or those who need easily digested nourishing food. If liked, 1 tablespoon brandy can be stirred in at the last minute.

BARK FAN
BOILED RICE

Preparation time　10 minutes
Cooking time　　30 minutes
To serve　　　　4-5

You will need

6-8 oz. Louisiana or Siam rice*
water

Boiled rice

* If packaged long-grained rice is used follow directions on packet.

Turn the rice into a large bowl and cover it well with cold water. Rub the rice between the thumb and fingers to remove loose starch. Drain off the water and repeat this treatment several times. Drain again. Place the bowl of rice under the cold water tap and let the water trickle on to it until overflowing and clear. Turn the drained rice into a large saucepan and add cold water to come to a depth of an inch above it. Cover and do not remove the lid during the cooking. Place over a high heat. After 3-4 minutes, lower the heat a little and lower it again after a further 3-4 minutes. Allow another 20 minutes at this low heat. With a fork, loosen the rice at the sides to allow steam to escape. Transfer to a heated serving dish.

NOR MEI FAN

STICKY RICE WITH SHRIMPS

Preparation time   overnight plus 10-15 minutes
Cooking time   1 hour
To serve   2-3

You will need

5 oz. pudding (round) rice
2 oz. dried shrimps (see page 151)
2 oz. lean roast pork
1 spring onion
1 dessertspoon pork dripping
pinch each sugar and Ve-Tsin (see page 151)
½ teaspoon ginger sherry (see page 151)

Soak the rice overnight.
Soak the shrimps for 3 minutes and steam them for 3 minutes.
Drain the rice and tie it loosely in a piece of butter muslin (cheese cloth) or mutton cloth (closely knitted cotton obtainable from the haberdashery departments of most stores). Steam it for 30 minutes. Remove. With the finger tips sprinkle generously with cold water and return to the steamer for a further 30 minutes.
Meanwhile dice the pork and finely chop the onion. Gently cook the onion in the pork dripping for 1 minute. Add the pork, seasonings and ginger sherry and cook for ½ minute, stirring all the time. Remove the rice from its bag. Turn it into a heated dish and add the shrimp and pork mixture. Stir together and serve.

YU PIN JUCK

'SOUPY' RICE WITH SOLE

Preparation time   6-8 minutes
Cooking time   3 hours
To serve   2-3

You will need

2 tablespoons round rice, well washed
1 piece dried tangerine peel (1 inch in diameter)
1 slice fresh ginger
2 pints (U.S. 5 cups) boiling water
peanut oil
fillets 1 small sole
1 teaspoon cornflour
pinch each salt and Ve-Tsin (see page 151)
1 dessertspoon beaten egg
½ teaspoon ginger sherry (see page 151)
1 oz. rice noodles

Turn rice into 3-pint saucepan. Add peel, ginger, water and 2 teaspoons peanut oil. Cook gently for 3 hours, stirring occasionally. Cut sole diagonally into thin slices. Place in bowl with cornflour, seasonings, beaten egg and sherry; work the mixture into them. When cooked, remove peel and ginger from rice add sole; cook for 2 minutes. Put noodles into hot deep oil for ½ minute, keeping them submerged with a shallow ladle. Divide the 'soupy' rice into 2-3 bowls. Sprinkle the lightly crushed rice noodles over soup and serve.

Note
This is like 'soupy' rice with beef (see page 128).

CHAR SHIU BOW
ROAST PORK DUMPLINGS

Preparation time 15-20 minutes
Cooking time 20 minutes
To serve 5

You will need

2-3 tablespoons lean roast pork
1 dessertspoon peanut oil
few drops soy sauce
pinch each salt, sugar and Ve-Tsin
  (see page 151)
¾ teaspoon cornflour
3 tablespoons cold water
1 teaspoon oyster sauce

DOUGH

4 oz. plain flour
¼ teaspoon baking powder
1 level dessertspoon sugar
2 tablespoons peanut oil
1 tablespoon water

Chop the pork fairly finely and fry it in the oil for under a minute, tossing it about. Add the soy sauce, seasonings and ½ teaspoon of cornflour, blended with the water, and cook, stirring, for 1½ minutes. (This is a rather dryish mixture.) Set aside to become cold.

Mix together the remaining cornflour and the oyster sauce and add to the meat. Divide the mixture into 5 equal portions.

TO MAKE THE DOUGH

Turn the flour, baking powder and sugar on to a pastry board. Make a hole in the centre. Pour the oil and water into it and gradually mix together with the handle of a wooden spoon. Gather up the dough and knead it very well, using the heels of the hands, until it is very firm. Divide into 5 balls and flatten each into a round 2½ inches in diameter. Place one round of dough in one hand. Add a portion of the filling and bring the outer edges together and pinch them with the thumb and forefinger of the other hand *(see photograph 1)*. Continue this pinching and shaping all round to form the dumplings *(see photograph 2)*.

Place each dumpling on a square of greaseproof paper and steam for 20 minutes.

LAP CHUNG KIN
STEAMED CHINESE
SAUSAGE ROLL

Preparation time 10-15 minutes
Cooking time 20 minutes
To serve 3-4

You will need

4 oz. self-raising flour
1 level dessertspoon sugar
1 teaspoon melted lard
1 tablespoon water
2 Chinese dried sausages (see note opposite)

Roast pork dumplings (1)

Roast pork dumplings (2)

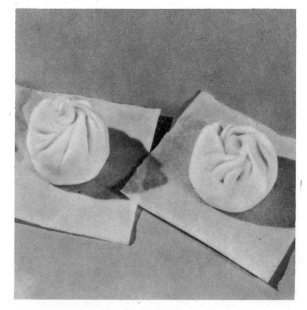

First, make the dumpling paste.

Sift the flour and sugar on to an enamelled tray. Make a small hole in the centre and pour the liquid but cool lard and the water into it.

With the tip of a finger or the handle of a wooden spoon gradually draw the flour mixture into the centre to make a firmish dough. (It may need a trifle more water.) When all is well mixed together, begin to knead with the heel of the hand to produce a firm and well blended dough.

Form the dough into a roll and set it aside.

Wipe the sausages with a cloth wrung out of hot water.

Halve each, lengthwise, making 4 slices.

Cut across the roll of dough to make 4 equal-sized pieces.

Roll each out to the length of the halved sausages. Place a piece of sausage on each and roll up, pressing lightly to seal the joins.

Place the rolls, join side down, on a lightly oiled plate, put in a steamer and steam for 20 minutes. Remove and serve.

Note

Chinese dried sausages are available during cold weather from dealers in Chinese and oriental supplies.

Roast pork dumplings (3)

GEE YUK DAN BOW

PORK AND EGG DUMPLINGS

Preparation time   15-20 minutes
Cooking time   20 minutes
To serve   2-4

You will need

NOODLE PASTE

3 oz. self-raising flour
1 teaspoon sugar
1 teaspoon melted lard
1 very small egg

FILLING

4 oz. pork, chopped, with a little fat in it
1 dessertspoon water chestnuts, chopped
1 dessertspoon bamboo shoots, chopped
pinch each salt, sugar, pepper and Ve-Tsin (see page 151)
$\frac{1}{2}$ teaspoon ginger sherry (see page 151)
1 teaspoon beaten egg
$\frac{1}{2}$ teaspoon cornflour
4 hard-boiled eggs, shelled

TO MAKE THE NOODLE PASTE

Sift the flour and sugar on to an enamelled tray. Make a well in the centre and add the cool melted lard and the egg to it. Gradually work the flour into the liquid and knead very well. Cover and set aside.

TO MAKE THE FILLING

Mix pork, chestnut and bamboo shoots; chop again. Add seasonings, sherry and beaten egg. Work together. Work in cornflour.

Divide the noodle paste into 4 equal-sized pieces. Form each into a ball and then spread it out with the heel of the hand to a 4-inch round. Form the meat mixture into 4 little rounds. Place a shelled egg, point down, on each and work the meat mixture up and around it to cover it completely.

Place each meat-coated egg, lengthwise, in the centre of each round of noodle paste. Gather the surrounding paste up and over. Pinch the joins together. *(See step-by-step photographs on page 130.)* Place each 'dumpling' on a small square of grease-proof paper on a plate. Put it in a steamer and steam for 20 minutes.

Serve at once.

HAR GOW
STEAMED PRAWN DUMPLINGS

Preparation time   7-8 minutes
Cooking time   20 minutes
To serve   3-6 dumplings

You will need

2 tablespoons raw pork
1 Pacific prawn
1 dessertspoon Chinese mushrooms
  (see page 150)
1 tablespoon canned bamboo shoots
good pinch Ve-Tsin (see page 151)
pinch salt
½ teaspoon ginger sherry
  (see page 151)
few drops sesame oil
3 oz. Chinese wheat starch
hot water

Cut the pork into smallish pieces. Clean the prawn and cut it up. Chop the mushrooms and the bamboo shoots.
Mix them together and pound them into a paste. Add the seasonings, sherry and sesame oil. Work all together and place ready.
Heap the wheat starch on an enamelled tray. Make a depression in the centre and add hot water, drop by drop, to make a firmish paste. Place it in a basin and steam it for 5 minutes.
Remove and form into a roll as soon as it can be easily handled.
Cut into 6 equal-sized pieces, about 1¼-inches each. With the flat of a chopper, press each into rounds 2½-inches in diameter.
Divide the filling between them, rounding the top of each portion.
Pinch the edges together into a Dutch bonnet shape.
Steam for 15 minutes, transfer to a heated dish and serve.

Note

The dumplings must be completed while the paste is still warm; otherwise, they will not hold together.

SHUNG TUNG GOW GEE
SHRIMP CRESCENT DUMPLINGS

Preparation time   15-20 minutes
Cooking time   20 minutes
To serve   2-4

You will need

NOODLE DOUGH
3 oz. self-raising flour
1 teaspoon sugar
1 teaspoon melted lard, cooled
1 very small egg

FILLING
2 oz. peeled cooked shrimps
2 oz. raw pork, finely chopped
1 tablespoon chopped Chinese mushrooms
  (see page 150)
1 tablespoon canned bamboo shoots
pinch each salt, sugar and Ve-Tsin
  (see page 151)
½ teaspoon ginger sherry (see page 151)
few drops sesame oil
½ teaspoon cornflour
peanut oil for frying

TO MAKE THE NOODLE DOUGH

Sift flour and sugar on to enamelled tray. Make a well in centre; drop lard and egg into it. Gradually mix in flour. Knead well until dough is firm and evenly blended.

TO MAKE THE FILLING

Turn the shrimps into a basin. Add the finely chopped pork, chopped mushrooms and bamboo shoots, seasonings, sherry, sesame oil and cornflour. Mix all well together. Divide the noodle dough into 4 equal portions. Gradually flatten them with the heel of the hand into 3½- to 4-inch rounds. Divide the filling between them, placing a portion on one half of each round. Fold over, turn in the ends and gather and pinch the joins together. Place each on a piece of greaseproof paper on a plate. Place it in the steamer and steam for 20 minutes. Remove, lower them into shallow hot oil and fry on both sides to colour a little.

Chicken, ham and prawn omelet

Chicken, ham, bamboo shoots and mushroom omelet

EGGS AND GARNISHES

DAN; FUI CHOY

In this small section, there are some very interesting Chinese omelets.
Try them. They make for such variety as you may not have met with before.

The Chinese use garnishes a great deal in their food. Besides watercress and the attractive onion flowers, shredded omelet and ham make excellent garnishes.

SANG CHUNG JING DAN
STEAMED EGGS
WITH SPRING ONION

Preparation time   2-3 minutes
Cooking time   15 minutes
To serve   2-3

You will need

1 teaspoon finely chopped spring onion
pinch each salt and Ve-Tsin
  (see page 151)
few shakes white pepper
few drops ginger sherry
  (see page 151)
few drops sesame oil
2 eggs
2 tablespoons cold water

Turn the onion into a basin.
Add the seasonings, sherry and sesame oil and work them together.
Break the eggs into the basin and add the water. Whip to a froth with a rotary whisk or electric mixer.
Turn into an oiled basin, filling it only two-thirds full. Place in a steamer and steam for 15 minutes. (There is no need to cover the basin.)
Unmould and serve.

GAI DAN CHAR
EGG TEA

Preparation time   3-4 minutes
Cooking time   30-35 minutes
To serve   3

You will need

2-3 tablespoons lotus seeds (see page 151)*
2 tablespoons white rock sugar
¾ pint (U.S. 1⅞ cups) water
3 eggs
* Buy lotus seeds already halved with their central germs removed. Canned lotus seeds can also be bought.

Drop the lotus seeds into a pan with the sugar and water, bring to the boil and simmer until the seeds are soft.
Meanwhile soft-boil and shell the eggs.
Remove the lotus seeds and peel off their skins.
Return the seeds to the syrup and add the eggs, still remaining whole.
Heat through.
Turn all into a deep heated dish and serve at once.

Note
These eggs are eaten with a spoon, a little of them at a time being eaten with a portion of the lotus seeds.

GAI SEE CHOW DAN

BEAN SPROUTS AND
BAMBOO SHOOTS OMELET

Preparation time   3-4 minutes
Cooking time   4-5 minutes
To serve   2-3

You will need

2 tablespoons bean sprouts (see page 102)
1 tablespoon canned bamboo shoots
1 spring onion
2 eggs
1 dessertspoon peanut oil
1 teaspoon pork dripping
pinch each salt and Ve-Tsin (see page 151)
few shakes white pepper
½ teaspoon ginger sherry (see page 151)
few drops sesame oil
1 tablespoon hot chicken stock

Pick over the bean sprouts, discarding any seed pods. Cut the bamboo shoots into thin strips. Cut the spring onion lengthwise, then into short lengths. Chop these finely and keep them apart. Beat the eggs.
Heat together the oil and pork dripping in a frying-pan. Add the bean sprouts and bamboo shoots and fry them for 1 minute. Add the seasonings, sherry, sesame oil and stock and cook for 1 minute, tossing the vegetables about.

Turn the beaten eggs into this mixture and as soon as it will come together form into an omelet.
Turn on to a heated serving dish. Sprinkle with the finely chopped onion and serve at once.

HUNG YEN CHOW DAN

ALMOND OMELET

Preparation time   less than 1 minute
Cooking time   2½-3 minutes
To serve   2

You will need

1 tablespoon almonds
1 tablespoon peanut oil
2 beaten eggs
tiny pinch each salt, sugar and Ve-Tsin
   (see page 151)
parsley

Cut the almonds into slivers or roughly chop them.
Heat the oil in a frying-pan. Add the eggs and stir them so rapidly that they are at once mixed.
As quickly as possible add the three seasonings and the almonds and spread them out.
Roll the omelet and turn it on to a warm oval plate — not a hot one because the omelet would go on cooking and become hard. Garnish with parsley and serve at once.

Almond omelet

Eggs in sweet-sour sauce

DIM SIN CHOW DAN
EGGS IN SWEET-SOUR SAUCE

Preparation time   2-3 minutes
Cooking time   7-8 minutes
To serve   2

You will need

1 dessertspoon peanut oil
1 dessertspoon raw white cabbage
1 dessertspoon raw carrot
1 slice fresh ginger
3 dessertspoons peanut oil
2 eggs
parsley

SAUCE

$\frac{1}{4}$ pint (U.S. $\frac{5}{8}$ cup) water
1 crushed clove garlic
1 dessertspoon peanut oil
2 tablespoons sugar
1 teaspoon tomato purée
2 tablespoons malt vinegar
salt to taste
1 teaspoon cornflour
1 dessertspoon cold water

Cut the cabbage, carrot and ginger into thin strips and have them ready.
To make the sauce, mix the first seven ingredients together in a small pan. Bring to the boil. Add the cornflour, blended with the water, and boil for $1\frac{1}{2}$ minutes.
Heat a dessertspoon of oil in another pan. Add the

vegetables and ginger and cook over a medium heat for 1 minute.
Strain the sauce through a sieve on to them and keep hot.
Heat 2 dessertspoons of oil in a frying-pan. Break 1 egg into it. It will very quickly brown on the underside. Fold it over in a half circle and, away from the heat, finish the cooking. Lift with a fish slice into a heated dish. Cook the other egg in the same way. Place it beside the first egg and cover with the sauce and vegetables.
Garnish with parsley and serve.

HAR MEI CHOW DAN
SCRAMBLED EGGS WITH DRIED SHRIMPS

Preparation time   3-4 minutes
Cooking time   2-3 minutes
To serve   2-3

You will need

2 tablespoons dried shrimps (see page 151)
2 eggs
salt and Ve-Tsin (see page 151)
white pepper
2 teaspoons peanut oil
generous pinch sugar
$\frac{1}{2}$ teaspoon ginger sherry (see page 151)
few drops sesame oil
1 teaspoon finely chopped spring onion green

Cover the shrimps generously with boiling water and leave for 3 minutes.
Beat the eggs with a tiny pinch each of salt, Ve-Tsin and a few shakes pepper.
Drain the shrimps and rinse them to dislodge any sand.
Heat 1 teaspoon oil in a small frying-pan. Add the shrimps, another pinch salt, Ve-Tsin, few shakes pepper, sugar, sherry and sesame oil and cook for 1 minute.
Heat the remaining oil in another pan. Add the beaten eggs.
Turn the hot shrimps on top and stir together to form into an omelet roll.
Turn on to a heated dish, sprinkle with the chopped onion green and serve.

Folding an omelet before shredding

SHREDDED OMELET

Shredded omelet is used for garnishing. It is wafer-thin. Beat 1 egg. Heat 1 teaspoon peanut oil in a frying-pan and pour in just enough egg to cover the bottom of the pan when it is turned this way and that. Cook until firm and at once transfer to a surface rubbed with a smear of oil.

TO SHRED THE OMELET

Fold it as shown in the photograph then cut it into thin strips and use where indicated.

Shredded omelet, shredded ham and watercress

LO SUEY DAN
SOYA EGGS

Preparation time   3-4 minutes
Cooking time   about 1¾ hours
To serve   2-3

You will need

2 eggs
1 clove garlic
4 thin slices fresh ginger
2 spring onions
1 teaspoon peanut oil
¾ pint (U.S. 1⅞ cups) hot chicken stock
3 tablespoons light-toned soy sauce
2 tablespoons dark soy sauce
pinch caraway seeds
pinch aniseeds

If the eggs have been stored in the refrigerator, remove them long enough in advance so that they acquire room temperature. Lower them into gently boiling water which should be deep enough to cover them and give them 15-20 minutes boiling, depending on their size.
While the eggs are cooking, crush the garlic, ginger and spring onions. Heat the oil in a frying-pan and fry them in it till a golden colour. Discard them. Add to the pan the chicken stock, the pale and dark soy sauces and the seeds, tied in a piece of muslin, and heat through. After removing the shells, make a deep cross in each egg. Place them in a small pan and pour the sauce over them. Cover and cook very gently for 1½ hours at almost lower than simmering point. Remove the bag of seeds. Quarter the eggs, lengthwise, and serve hot with boiled rice (see page 128) or cold in the remaining sauce.

Note

By the end of 1½ hours, the eggs will have absorbed the soy sauces and the flavour will have completely entered them.

SHREDDED HAM

In the Chinese kitchen shredded ham is often sprinkled over other food at the last minute. This garnish consists of lean boiled ham, cut into thin slices and then chopped as finely as possible.

Steamed omelet

GEE YUK JING DAN
STEAMED OMELET

Preparation time   2-3 minutes
Cooking time   15-20 minutes
To serve   2-3

You will need

2 tablespoons raw lean pork
1 tablespoon canned water chestnuts
2-3 spring onions, depending on size
small pinch each salt, sugar and Ve-Tsin
   (see page 151)
2 beaten eggs

Very finely chop the pork, chestnuts and onions. Add the three seasonings and mix together on a plate.
Very sparingly oil a shallow heatproof dish, about 6 inches in diameter. Sprinkle the meat mixture into it and very carefully pour in the eggs so as not to disturb it. Place in the steamer and gently steam for 15-20 minutes.

YIM KOK DAN
SALT-BAKED EGGS

Preparation time   1-2 minutes
Cooking time   25 minutes
To serve   2-3

You will need

kitchen salt
2-3 eggs

Although 'baking' generally refers to oven cooking, the eggs in this case are baked on top of the stove. The eggs must be at room temperature.
The quantity of salt used depends on the size of the pan and the number of eggs to be cooked in it. For 2-3 eggs, 1 lb. salt may be enough.
Turn enough cold salt into the pan to form a good base for the eggs. Make 2-3 dimples in it and place an egg in each, having at least ½-inch of salt under them. Cover completely with further salt. Very gently heat through and keep the eggs moving with a spoon. Increase the heat slightly. The eggs will require 25 minutes of this slow 'baking'. Remove; shell the eggs and serve them.

Note

Make sure that the eggs rest on a base of salt and not touching the bottom of the pan because, if they do, they will break during the cooking.
While the pan need not be a large one, there must be space in it to enable the eggs to be moved about.

DAI GEE CHOW DAN
SCALLOP OMELET

Preparation time   4-5 minutes
Cooking time   5-6 minutes
To serve   2-3

You will need

3 small scallops (white only)
tiny piece fresh ginger
tiny piece garlic
2 dessertspoons peanut oil
1 teaspoon chopped onion
pinch each salt and Ve-Tsin (see page 151)
2 shakes white pepper
few drops ginger sherry (see page 151)
2 beaten eggs

Wash the scallops in running water. Trim and cut them into not-too-small dice. Place them ready. Crush the ginger and garlic.
Heat 1 dessertspoon of the oil in a frying-pan. Add the ginger, garlic and onion and cook for 1 minute. Add the scallops, seasonings and ginger sherry and cook for 2 minutes. Turn on to a dish. Wipe out the frying-pan. Heat remaining oil in it. Add beaten eggs and then the scallops and move them about. Form into a roll. Put on heated dish and serve.

Chinese pickles

SUB GUM GEUNG

CHINESE PICKLES

These are a mixture of carrots, ginger, small whole onions and various other ingredients.
They can be bought at any Chinese emporium and in departmental stores where a good supply of Chinese materials is stocked.

YOW KOUN SOUNG

GARLIC-GINGER SAUCE

Preparation time   6 minutes
Cooking time   6 minutes

You will need

1-2 cloves garlic
5 thin slices fresh ginger (see below)
2-3 spring onions
3 tablespoons peanut oil
salt to taste
dash soy sauce

Skin the cloves of garlic.
Crush and chop them.
Cut the ginger into thin strips and the onions into 1½-2-inch lengths.
Heat the oil.
Cook the garlic in it till pale gold. Add the ginger and onions and cook very gently for a few minutes.
Season with salt to taste.
Sprinkle with the soy sauce.

Note

Fresh ginger is different from the dried root ginger as it is moist and almost juicy.
It is cut into slices or shreds and either cooked in oil until a pale golden colour and then discarded or left in the dish with the other ingredients.

GEUNG CHO NGAP

GINGER-VINEGAR SAUCE

Preparation time   few minutes
No cooking
To serve   up to 6-7

You will need

1 tablespoon very finely chopped fresh ginger
1 teaspoon chopped spring onion
3 tablespoons malt vinegar
1 good teaspoon sugar
good pinch each salt and Ve-Tsin (see page 151)
dash Tabasco sauce
½ teaspoon plum sauce (see page 151)
few shakes pepper

Blend all the above ingredients together. Turn the mixture into a sauce-boat and hand it separately. This sauce is for roast duck.

Garlic-ginger sauce

140

GAI SEE CHOW DAN

CHICKEN, HAM, BAMBOO SHOOTS AND MUSHROOM OMELET

(Illustrated in colour on page 134)

Preparation time   9-10 minutes
Cooking time   3-4 minutes
To serve   4

You will need

2 tablespoons skinned roast chicken
1 tablespoon boiled ham
1 tablespoon bamboo shoots
1 cooked Chinese mushroom (see page 150)
1 tomato
2-3 tablespoons strips lettuce
4 radishes
4 eggs
pinch salt
tiny pinch pepper
¼ teaspoon ginger sherry*
2 tablespoons chicken stock
1 dessertspoon peanut oil

GARNISH

lettuce, tomato slices and radishes

* Cut 2 oz. fresh ginger into thin strips. Put into a bottle and cover with half a bottle warm brown sherry. Leave to infuse, strain.

Cut the chicken, ham and bamboo shoots into match-sticks. Slice the mushroom and tomato. Cut the lettuce into strips and make 'lilies' of the radishes. With a sharp small pliable knife, make shallow cuts from the top of each and then cut down a little more than half-way behind the skin, leaving it intact and the centre like a round 'bud'. Drop the radishes into ice-cold water and the 'petals' will expand. Beat the eggs just enough to blend the yolks and whites. Add the chicken, ham, bamboo shoots, mushroom, seasoning, sherry and chicken stock.

Heat the oil in a frying-pan. Turn the mixture into it and quickly move it about with the back of a large spoon, first dipped in oil, without breaking it up. Cook the omelet as you like — very soft and barely set inside or a little more set. Form it into the usual roll.

Have a bed of lettuce on a serving dish. Turn the omelet on to it and garnish with the tomato slices and the radishes.

BARK DOW DAN

CHICKEN, HAM AND PRAWN OMELET

(Illustrated in colour on page 133)

Preparation time   8-10 minutes
Cooking time   5-6 minutes
To serve   3-4

You will need

1½ tablespoons peanut oil
1 chopped small onion
2-3 tablespoons bean sprouts, picked over
1 tablespoon cooked chicken*
1 tablespoon boiled ham*
1 tablespoon shelled cooked prawns*
1 tablespoon canned bamboo shoots*
1-2 white unopened cultivated mushrooms*
1 tablespoon cooked peas
pinch salt
pinch each sugar and Ve-Tsin
   (see page 151)
½ teaspoon ginger sherry (see page 151)
½ teaspoon sesame oil
few drops soy sauce
1 dessertspoon chicken stock
1 egg

THE SAUCE

¼ pint (U.S. ⅝ cup) chicken stock
1 tablespoon tomato sauce
pinch each salt and Ve-Tsin
½ teaspoon cornflour
1 dessertspoon water

* All thinly sliced.

Heat 1 tablespoon oil in omelet pan and cook onion for a few minutes. Add bean sprouts and cook ¼ minute. Add next 12 ingredients. Shake and toss over fairly high heat for 1-2 minutes, not frying the mixture but letting it cook in the steam created. Shape into a mound on a heated serving dish.

Heat ½ tablespoon of oil in another pan. Pour the egg, beaten with a tiny pinch of salt, into it and tilt the pan this way and that to spread the egg very thin. It is ready in less than ½ minute. Carefully lift it on top of the mound.

TO MAKE THE SAUCE

Bring the first 4 ingredients to the boil. Add the cornflour blended with the water and cook for a further minute. Pour the sauce over the egg when it will spread out and into the dish.

YUNG CHOW DAN
SPECIAL CHICKEN OMELET
(Illustrated in colour on opposite page)

Preparation time   8-10 minutes
Cooking time   8-10 minutes
To serve   3-4

You will need

1 tablespoon raw chicken
1 tablespoon raw pork
1 tablespoon water chestnuts
1 tablespoon cooked ham
1 tablespoon bamboo shoots
1 tablespoon canned awabi
1 tablespoon Chinese mushrooms (see page 150)
1 tablespoon cooked peas
1½ tablespoons peanut oil
1 chopped small onion
1 beaten egg
pinch each salt, sugar and Ve-Tsin
   (see page 151)
½ teaspoon ginger sherry (see page 151)
½ teaspoon sesame oil
few drops soy sauce
1 dessertspoon chicken stock

THE SAUCE

¼ pint (U.S. ⅝ cup) chicken stock
1 tablespoon tomato ketchup
pinch each salt, sugar and Ve-Tsin
½ teaspoon cornflour
1 dessertspoon water

Dice the chicken and pork and cut the water chestnuts, ham, bamboo shoots, awabi and mushroom into thin strips. Set these aside. Heat 1 tablespoon peanut oil in a frying-pan and fry the onion in it for 2-3 minutes. Add the chicken and pork and cook for 3-4 minutes, tossing them about. Add the ham, bamboo shoots, awabi and mushroom and cook them for 3 minutes. Meanwhile, heat the remaining peanut oil in another frying-pan. Add the beaten egg, lightly seasoned with salt, and turn it this way and that to coat the bottom of the pan evenly. Cook for less than ½ minute, then remove from the heat.

Add to the main mixture the seasonings, sherry, sesame oil, soy sauce and chicken stock.

TO MAKE THE SAUCE

Bring the stock and ketchup to the boil. Add the seasonings and then stir in the cornflour, blended with the water, and cook for 1½ minutes.
Then add the peas to the main mixture and warm through. Turn the mixture into a heated serving dish and carefully place the cooked egg on top. Pour the sauce over it and serve.

FOO YUNG HAI
CRAB OMELET
(Illustrated in colour on opposite page)

Preparation time   5-6 minutes
Cooking time   4-5 minutes
To serve   2-3

You will need

2 tablespoons canned white crab meat
2 tablespoons canned bamboo shoots
½ tablespoon peanut oil
2 tablespoons bean sprouts
pinch salt
pinch sugar
pinch Ve-Tsin (see page 151)
½ teaspoon ginger sherry (see page 151)
½ teaspoon sesame oil
1 dessertspoon cornflour
1-2 tablespoons chicken stock
2 beaten eggs
1 tablespoon thinly cut boiled ham
sliced cucumber and tomato garnish

Flake the crab meat and thinly cut in strips the bamboo shoots. Heat the peanut oil in an omelet pan.
Add the crab meat, bamboo shoots, bean sprouts, salt, sugar, Ve-Tsin, sherry, sesame oil, cornflour and stock and cook for 1 minute.
Stir in the beaten eggs and cook for a further ½ minute. Sprinkle the ham down the centre and fold the omelet in half. Slide it on to a heated serving dish and garnish with the sliced cucumber and tomatoes.

142

Special chicken omelet; crab omelet

Melon surprise; Chinese preserved fruit

DESSERTS AND TEA

TIM BAN; CHA

The Chinese dessert we know best is chow chow, a delicious mixture of fruits — and even vegetables — prepared in a heavy syrup. It can be bought at any store stocking oriental foods.

There is a great number of teas from China because the shrub is grown in most parts of that vast country. Probably the ones that we know best are Lapsang Souchong (a superior blend described as having a 'smoky flavour'), Formosa Oolong (which has something of the aroma of ripe peaches) and Jasmine tea (perfumed with the fragrance of the jasmine flowers). Earl Grey is a delicately scented blend and a great favourite at tea-time.

It is difficult to decide between these teas. Jasmine is, perhaps, the most refreshing.

The Chinese way of making tea in a pot is the same as ours. The pot, always a china one, is scalded and drained. The tea is added to it — ½-1 teaspoon for each serving, depending on how much water is to be added to dilute it. It is then left to infuse for 5-6 minutes.

This dilution needs to be explained. A little tea is poured into each cup and the cups are then filled up with hot water. The Chinese add neither milk nor sugar to their tea. It may be mentioned here that Chinese tea-cups have no handles.

Another way of making Chinese tea is to put a few choice leaves into individual cups, add a little boiling water, cover the cup with a saucer, allow to infuse for a few minutes and then fill up with boiling water.

For the benefit of young housewives, a note on the storage of tea may not be amiss.

China tea, like teas in general, is peculiarly sensitive to other aromas. For this reason, it should be kept in a caddy with a tightly fitting lid. If stored in a loose-lidded caddy along with other things in a cupboard, it will absorb such aromas as they may have so that its own flavour is destroyed.

I well remember a good old-time grocer (rarely met with nowadays, alas!) who would never pack tea with other goods in a customer's shopping basket. Instead, he would wrap it up securely and tie it with a good loop so that it swung clear of other purchases. This was to prevent the contamination to which I have referred.

KUMQUATS OR CUMQUATS

These are little orange-like fruits — both in colour and flavour.

Kumquats are plum-sized and, like chow chow, are prepared in heavy syrup.

Cans of kumquats are available at any Chinese or oriental emporium.

LYCHEES

Occasionally lychees can be bought fresh. Usually they come to us in canned form from China. The fresh lychees have a thin but tough 'shell'. When this is removed, there is a white fruit with a black stone — but the canned ones are already stoned. Canned lychees come in a thin syrup. Their delicious flavour is difficult to describe.

In melon surprise (see page 148) the lychees are very attractive when their stone cavities are filled with green or red sweet cocktail cherries.

GINGER IN SYRUP

This needs no explanation. It can be bought at any of the stores and from most good-class grocers.

GEUNG BENG

GINGER BISCUITS

Preparation time   15 minutes
Cooking time   20 minutes
To make   16-20 biscuits

You will need

1 lb. plain flour
$\frac{1}{4}$ teaspoon baking powder
8 oz. lard
8 oz. castor sugar
1 heaped tablespoon finely chopped ginger
   (in syrup)
1 egg
few drops almond essence
32-40 small slivers ginger

Sift the flour and baking powder. Rub the lard into them, then add the castor sugar and chopped ginger, and then the egg, beaten with the almond essence.
Mix thoroughly together.
Form into 16-20 balls, flatten them slightly and place them on baking sheets, first smeared with lard. Lightly press 2 strips of ginger on each biscuit. Bake for 5 minutes at 425°F. or Gas Mark 7. Reduce the heat to 350°F. or Gas Mark 4 and bake for a further 15 minutes.
Remove to wire trays. When cold, store in an airtight tin.

Ginger biscuits

Rice sticks with chow chow

CHOW CHOW SHA HO FUN

RICE STICKS WITH CHOW CHOW

Preparation time   2 minutes
Cooking time   10 minutes
To serve   2-3

You will need

2-3 oz. rice sticks
3-4 tablespoons chow chow (see page 147)

Drop the rice sticks into plenty of boiling water and cook them for 10 minutes. Drain them and pour cold water over them. Drain the chow chow, reserving the syrup. Cut the chow chow into strips, holding back one piece for final garnish. Turn the well drained rice sticks into a serving dish. Cover with the strips of chow chow and sprinkle the syrup over all. Garnish with the piece reserved for the purpose.

YIT BIEN

MOON CAKES

These delicious little cakes, decorated with coloured sugar depicting rabbits, frogs and pagodas, are served at the Festival of the Moon in the Chinese calendar (approximately August 15).
They are generally bought ready to eat because of the number of ingredients required, some of which are not always easy to obtain. Further, their preparation and putting together are usually left to the specialist.

Moon cakes

The outside — that is, the crust — is not unlike that of a pork pie.
The filling is composed of sesame seeds, crushed peanuts and sugar candy, among other things. Many people think that they taste very much like marzipan.

Note

The moon cakes, when required, should be ordered well in advance from any good Chinese emporium.

JAR NGAR CHU
CANDIED BANANA FRITTERS

Preparation time   up to 6 minutes
Cooking time   3-4 minutes
To serve   4

You will need

3 oz. plain flour
pinch salt
½ beaten egg
water
6 tablespoons sugar
4 small ripe bananas*
peanut oil for deep frying
4 small bowls ice-cold water

* Choose really ripe bananas with skins that are brown-flecked.

First make the batter. Sift the flour and salt into a basin. Make a hole in the centre. Drop the half egg and ⅛ pint (U.S. ⅞ cup) water into it and gradually beat them together. Leave to rest for a little. Next,

prepare the syrup. Very slowly melt the sugar in 3 tablespoons water in a small strong pan. When it is dissolved, boil very hard until the syrup is a very pale straw colour. Have a folded cold wet cloth at hand. At this point, place the pan on it to arrest further cooking. Skin and scrape the bananas. Halve them lengthwise, then cut them across to make four portions per half banana. Dip them into the batter. Drain them, then drop them, one at a time, into the very hot oil and cook them for not more than a minute. Place them separately and in one layer in a hot buttered silver dish.
Reheat the syrup and carefully pour it over the bananas. Rush them to table where each person will take his or her share and drop them one at a time into the cold water when the surfaces will crystallise in the most delightful 'bubbles'.

Note

Practise this before serving to guests because it has to be speedily made.
At the best, the bananas are crisp. Failing this, they are still deliciously coated banana fritters.

CHOW CHOW
CHINESE PRESERVED FRUITS

A well-known mixture of melon, ginger, cumquats and pineapple, together with other Chinese fruits and vegetables preserved in thick syrup.

Candied banana fritters

SAI GWAR JUNG
MELON SURPRISE

(Illustrated in colour on page 144)

Preparation time   30 minutes
No cooking
To serve   6-8

You will need

1 honeydew melon of the size desired
1-2 peaches
1-2 pears
lemon juice
1 small can lychees
few green cocktail cherries in syrup
few red cocktail cherries in syrup
few cumquats (see page 145)
white wine to taste or 1 measure kirsch
  or framboise liqueur

With a long slender sharp-pointed knife, cut shallow 'V's all round the melon, about one-sixth way down from one end. Let the cuts reach right to the centre so that the top can be lifted off in one piece. Remove the seeds but retain the juice. With what is called a 'pomme noisette' (round or oval), scoop out the melon flesh, including that in the cut-off portion, into small balls or ovals. Peel and slice the peaches and cut the peeled and cored pears into small wedges.

Turn both in a little melon juice to prevent discoloration.

Place a green or red cherry in the stoned cavity of each lychee.

Mix together the melon balls or ovals, peach slices and pear wedges. Turn them into the melon 'shell'. Add the syrup from the lychees, wine to your own discretion or a measure of kirsch or framboise liqueur. Garnish with the stuffed lychees and the cumquats.

DRIED OLIVES AND PLUMS

These are salty-sweet and have a very particular function. Their main purpose is to induce saliva and, in this, they are wonderful!

You may be parched because you have eaten too well or drunk more spirits than are good for you and you may wake up with what is loosely termed a 'dehydrated mouth'. Just pop one of these olives or plums into it and at once the saliva flows and all discomfort disappears!

You can buy these olives and plums at any emporium dealing with oriental goods.

RED GINGER

This red ginger is very 'hot' and is for nibbling. It is one Chinese speciality that has not been and is not likely to be taken up to any extent by occidentals. I like it least of the above items but I suggest that you try it. It may appeal to you.

MELON SEEDS

These are, primarily, for Chinese people — in the same way as sunflower seeds are for Russians. There is a certain skill in nibbling the shells and extracting the kernels elegantly. Here again, I suggest trying them.

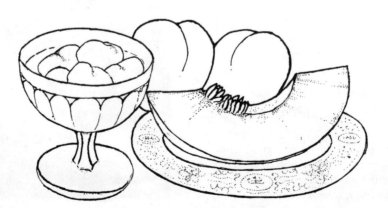

Dried olives, dried plums, red ginger and melon seeds

GLOSSARY

Owing to the increasing interest in Chinese cookery, many of the essential ingredients in the various dishes in this book are now stocked by the stores. Others — the more 'exotic' ones, perhaps — are obtainable from those establishments specialising in oriental supplies. In London, these are the Bombay Emporium, the Chinese Emporium and the Hong Kong Emporium. Of these, the Bombay Emporium has the most complete range. This firm exports much produce to all parts of the world. Amoy canned products, known the world over, are generally available from stores as well as 'emporia'.

Patna rice, from any grocer, is recommended but any long-grained American rice is ideal. Ve-Tsin is one brand of monosodium glutamate (see page 151).

It can be bought from the various 'emporia'. So can transparent noodles, long-life noodles, mungo bean sticks and dried Chinese mushrooms. In small cans are bamboo shoots, water chestnuts, red bean curd, black bean, yellow soy bean, Oyster sauce, soy sauce and sesame oil.

Chinese pickles are also obtainable. So are cans of chow chow (fruits, vegetables and ginger in syrup) and kumquats.

Stockists of Chinese food also sell dried prawns and salted cabbage.

Not every stockist has red food powder, but the Hong Kong Emporium sells it. This same establishment has also Chinese black eggs from time to time, but they are not always easily obtainable.

BIRDS' NESTS

These are very expensive. Whole nests are obtainable in 8-oz. packets. Broken nests, which many people use, cost a third of the price of the whole ones. Obtainable from emporia and stores stocking Chinese foods and cookery requirements.

BITTER MELON

This comes in cans and is more likely to be found in emporia specialising in Chinese goods than in other stores and shops.

BROWNED ALMONDS

Roast almonds appear in dishes such as chicken and almonds (see page 65) and are prepared as follows:

First, blanch round or Valencia-type almonds. Drop them into boiling water; leave for a minute, plunge into cold water and the skins can then be easily removed.

To brown them: Dry the almonds. Pour 2-3 tablespoons peanut oil into a suitably small pan. When fairly warm, add the blanched almonds and shake them over a fair heat so that they colour evenly. Lift on to absorbent kitchen paper with a perforated spoon.

CHICKEN STOCK

In many if not most of the savoury dishes in this book, chicken stock is an important ingredient. Supplies of this stock present no problem in the Chinese restaurant kitchen but in the normal home there is not always so much of it. There are, however, alternatives. Canned chicken consommé is one. Another to which we are more likely to resort, these days, is those very useful chicken cubes which are pretty generally available. A cube or part of one will make an acceptable 'stock'. Another source of chicken stock is the giblets which can be bought at little cost from many butchers and poulterers or delicatessen shops where many chicken are used. After reserving the livers for such dishes as chicken livers and cashew nuts (see page 24), make the stock with the remaining giblets in the usual way.

CHINESE DRIED SAUSAGES

These are obtainable during cold weather from dealers in Chinese and other oriental supplies.

CHINESE MUSHROOMS

These dried black mushrooms should be prepared a day in advance. Remove and discard the stalks. Soak the mushrooms overnight in water. Boil them for 6-10 minutes in chicken stock, drain them and they are ready to be used in any dish as directed in the recipe.

CHINESE MUSTARD PLANT

This can be obtained in cans from any emporium stocking Chinese and other oriental foods.

EGG NOODLES

These dried noodles come in 'rounds'. Many high-class grocers sell them. They can also be bought, of course, from most of the stores and establishments dealing in oriental goods.

FRESH GINGER

As distinct from the dried root ginger we know so well, fresh root ginger is moist and almost juicy. It is cut into slices or shreds and either cooked in oil until a pale gold colour and then discarded or left in the dish with its other ingredients.

GINGER (PRESERVED) IN SYRUP

Ginger in syrup, next to tea, must have been one of the first imports from China. All the stores and most good-class grocers stock it.

GINGER SHERRY

This is made in the kitchen. Cut 1-2 oz. fresh ginger into thin strips. Turn them into a bottle and cover with a warm brown sherry. Leave to infuse, strain and use as directed. For 2 oz. fresh ginger, ½ bottle sherry will be the right amount to add.

LOTUS SEEDS

These are mainly available in shops specialising in Chinese foods. They can be bought loose as well as prepared — that is, shelled, halved and with the centre germ removed.

LYCHEES

These arrive in this country in two forms — fresh and dried.

The stoned fresh lychees are obtainable in 20-oz. cans from all suppliers of Chinese products and also from most of the stores. They are also often to be found in local grocers' shops.

The dried lychees come in their thin brown shells. The dark rich flesh is somewhat raisin-like in appearance and the flavour resembles that of a muscat grape. Fruiterers as well as the above-mentioned stores stock them.

MUNGO BEAN STICKS

These, made from green bean flour, come in 1-lb. packages but are also obtainable in bulk at a lower price. Mainly obtainable from emporia specialising in oriental goods.

PLUM SAUCE

This comes in cans and is obtainable from the various emporia stocking Chinese and other oriental supplies. If it is difficult to obtain, one can make one's own by blending the syrup from Indian chutney with plum jam to produce a fairly thick sauce and then sieving it. The chutney syrup supplies the necessary condiments.

RED BEAN CURD

This comes in 6-oz. cans. Obtainable from stores and emporia dealing in Chinese food supplies.

TANGERINE PEEL

This is simply dried tangerine (mandarin or clementine) orange peel. It can be bought from the above-mentioned emporia as well as those departments of the stores where oriental products are stocked. But one can dry one's own.

I dry mine when the above oranges are available simply by putting the peel in the oven after it has been in use, with the heat switched off, and leave them to dry slowly in it.

SESAME SEEDS

Sesame seeds are found in stores other than those selling Chinese supplies; for instance, in places where Greek and Turkish foodstuffs are sold.

SHRIMPS AND PRAWNS (DRIED)

These are generally bought loose from stockists of oriental food supplies.

VE-TSIN OR MONOSODIUM GLUTAMATE

Ve-Tsin or monosodium glutamate, known briefly as 'M.S.G.', is derived from vegetable sources and, in appearance, resembles fine salt. Its purpose is to accentuate or enhance the flavour of foods, especially proteins, to which it is added. It is something of a 'magical' material which has become an important ingredient in innumerable packaged and canned foods. While it is of comparatively recent use in this country, it has been known to the Chinese and Japanese for hundreds of years, its original source being seaweed. In the early part of the present century, occidental chemists were able to extract monosodium glutamate from various vegetable proteins. It is available in this country under various proprietary names such as 'Accent' (made in U.S.A.), 'Aji No. Moto' (made in Japan), 'Mei Yen' (made by the Spice Islands Company of California) and 'Stress', (made in Great Britain). Ve-Tsin is the proprietary name of M.S.G. (made in Hong Kong).

Home cooks, in the wake of food manufacturers, are realising, more and more, the virtue of 'M.S.G.' under whatever name it is bought and it is growing in popularity. Like all seasonings and flavourings, 'a little goes a long way'. This calls for a certain discretion in its use.

YELLOW AND BLACK SOYA BEANS

Like red bean curd, these come in 6-oz. cans and can be bought from the same sources.

INDEX